Lay, Lady, Lay Bob Dylan 73

Let It Be The Beatles 76

Life On Mars? David Bowie 79

Love Story Taylor Swift 82

Make You Feel My Love Adele 86

Mrs. Robinson Simon & Garfunkel 88

Ordinary World Duran Duran 91

Redemption Song Bob Marley 94

Rocket Man Elton John 96

Romeo And Juliet Dire Straits 99

Save Tonight Eagle-Eye Cherry 102

The Scientist Coldplay 104

Sing Travis 107

The Sound of Silence Simon & Garfunkel 116

Space Oddity David Bowie 110

Stand By Me Ben E. King 114

Tears In Heaven Eric Clapton 119

Torn Natalie Imbruglia 122

Vincent (Starry Starry Night) Don McLean 124

The Weight The Band 128

Wild World Cat Stevens 131

Wonderwall Oasis 134

Yesterday The Beatles 140

You're Still The One Shania Twain 137

You've Got A Friend James Taylor 142

Ain't No Sunshine

Words & Music by Bill Withers

The Complete Guitar Player
Acoustic Songbook

Published by:
Wise Publications
14-15 Berners Street, London W1T 3LJ, UK.

Exclusive Distributors:
Music Sales Limited
Distribution Centre, Newmarket Road, Bury St Edmunds, Suffolk IP33 3YB, UK.
Music Sales Corporation
180 Madison Avenue, 24th Floor, New York NY 10016, USA.
Music Sales Pty Limited
Units 3-4, 17 Willfox Street, Condell Park, NSW 2200, Australia.

Compiled and edited by Toby Knowles.
Music processed by shedwork.com
Cover designed by Fresh Lemon.
Printed in the EU.

Your Guarantee of Quality
As publishers, we strive to produce every book to the highest commercial standards.
This book has been carefully designed to minimise awkward page turns and to make playing
from it a real pleasure.
Particular care has been given to specifying acid-free, neutral-sized paper made from
pulps which have not been elemental chlorine bleached. This pulp is from
farmed sustainable forests and was produced with special regard for the environment.
Throughout, the printing and binding have been planned to ensure a sturdy,
attractive publication which should give years of enjoyment.
If your copy fails to meet our high standards, please inform us and we will gladly replace it.

www.musicsales.com

Wise Publications
part of The Music Sales Group
London / New York / Paris / Sydney / Copenhagen / Berlin / Madrid / Hong Kong / Tokyo

The A Team Ed Sheeran 6

Ain't No Sunshine Bill Withers 4

Annie's Song John Denver 9

Brown Eyed Girl Van Morrison 12

California Dreamin' The Mamas And The Papas 15

The Cave Mumford & Sons 18

Chasing Pavements Adele 22

Don't Know Why Norah Jones 25

Don't Panic Coldplay 28

Dream Catch Me Newton Faulkner 30

Every Rose Has Its Thorn Poison 33

Father And Son Cat Stevens 36

Fields Of Gold Sting 39

Fifty Ways To Leave Your Lover Paul Simon 46

Folsom Prison Blues Johnny Cash 42

Friday I'm In Love The Cure 44

Hallelujah Jeff Buckley 49

Hey, Soul Sister Train 52

Ho Hey The Lumineers 55

Homeward Bound Simon & Garfunkel 60

I Will Wait Mumford & Sons 63

Imagine John Lennon 58

The Joker Steve Miller Band 66

Jolene Dolly Parton 70

Knockin' On Heaven's Door Bob Dylan 68

2. Won-der this___ time where she's

And I know, I know, I know,___ I know,

I know, I know, I know, I know, I know I know, I know, I know, I know, I know, I know,___

___ I know, I know, I know, I know, I know, I know, I know, I know, I know, I know, I

know, hey,___ I ought to leave the young thing a - lone,___ but, ain't no sun - shine when she's

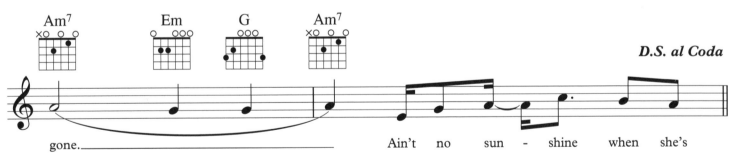

gone._____ Ain't no sun - shine when she's

An - y- time___ she goes a - way.

The A Team

Words & Music by Ed Sheeran

Picking style:

Capo: Fret 2

Intro

Verse

1. White lips___ pale face,___ breath-ing in___ snow - flakes.
2. Ripped gloves,___ rain - coat,___ tried to swim,___ stay a - float._

___ Burnt lungs, sour taste.___ Light's gone, day's end._
___ Dry house, wet clothes.___ Loose change, bank notes._

___ Strug-gl-ing___ to pay_ rent.___ Long nights, strange men.___
___ Wear-y-eyed, dry___ throat.___ Call girl,_ no phone.___

And they_

Chorus

___ say she's in the Class A___ team. Stuck in her day dream. Been this way_ since

Annie's Song

Words & Music by John Denver

Picking style:

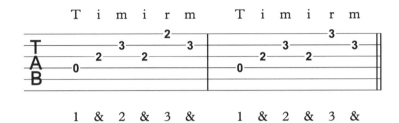

Intro

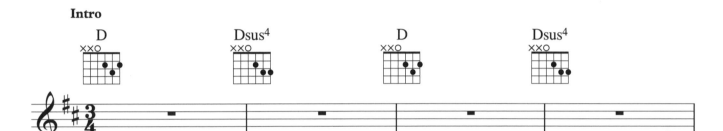

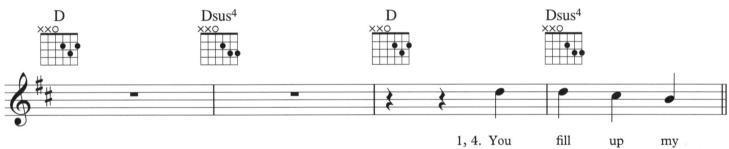

1, 4. You fill up my

Verse

(1, 4.) sen - ses   like a night in a
(2.) love_____ you,   let me give my life_____
(3.) mm,_____   mm,_____ mm,_____

for - est,_____   like the moun - tains in_____
to you._____   Let me drown in your
mm._____   Mm, mm,_____

- gain._____
- gain._____
- gain._____

2. Come,   let   me
3. Mm,   mm,_____
4. You   fill   up   my

Coda

(4.) des - ert,   like   a   sleep - y   blue

o - cean;_____   you   fill   up   my

sen - - ses,   come, fill   me   a -

- gain._____

Brown Eyed Girl

Words & Music by Van Morrison

Strumming style:

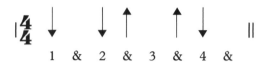

> Try to memorise the chord sequence. That way, you can concentrate on the sound, rather than reading, when you play this song.

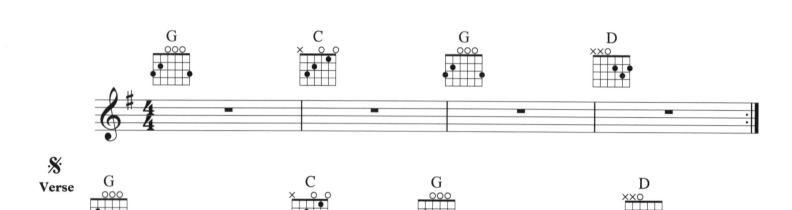

Verse

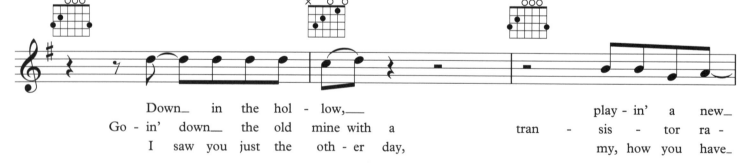

1. Hey where did we go,   days__ when the rains__ came?
2. What - ev - er hap-pened   to Tues-day and so____ slow?
3. So hard to find my way   now__ that I'm all on my own.

Down__ in the hol - low,__   play - in' a new__
Go - in' down__ the old mine with a   tran - sis - tor ra -
I saw you just the oth - er day,   my, how you have__

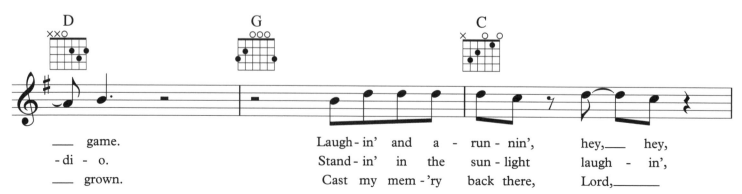

__ game.   Laugh - in' and a - run - nin', hey,__ hey,
-di - o.   Stand - in' in the sun - light laugh - in',
__ grown.   Cast my mem - 'ry back there, Lord,____

skip - pin' and   a - jump - in',   in   the   mis - ty   morn-
hid - in'   be - hind   a   rain - bow's wall,   slip - pin' and   a - slid -
some - times I'm   o - ver - come think - in' 'bout   it,   mak - in' love   in   the green_

- in'   fog___   with   our,   our hearts   a - thump - in' and you,_
- in'   all   a - long   the   wa - ter - fall   with   you,_
___ grass,   be hind   the   sta - di - um___   with you,_

___   my   brown eyed   girl.___
___   my   brown eyed   girl.___
___   my   brown eyed   girl.___

1.

You___ my___   brown eyed   girl.___

2.

To Coda

Do you___ re - mem - ber   when   we used   to sing?_

13

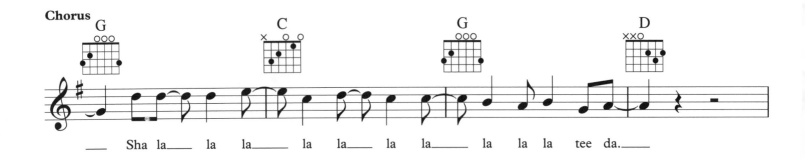

Sha la___ la la___ la la___ la la___ la la la tee da.___

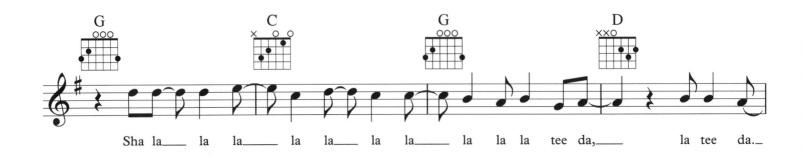

Sha la___ la la___ la la la la___ la la la tee da,___ la tee da.___

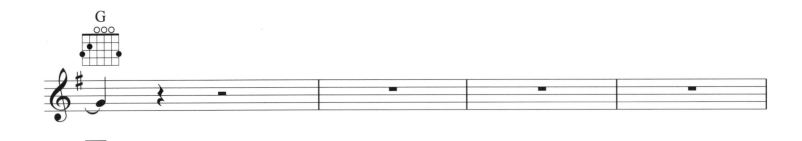

———

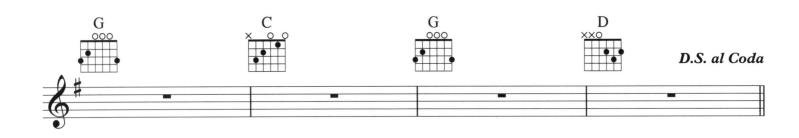

D.S. al Coda

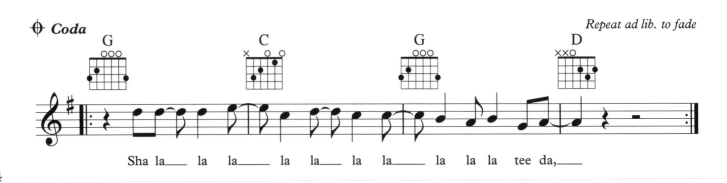

Repeat ad lib. to fade

✛ *Coda*

Sha la___ la la___ la la la la___ la la la tee da,___

California Dreamin'

Words & Music by John Phillips & Michelle Gilliam

Intro:

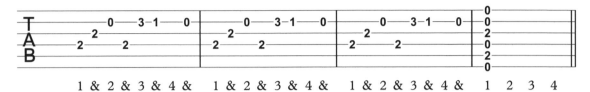

Strumming style:

Capo: Fret 4

1, 2. All the leaves are

Verse

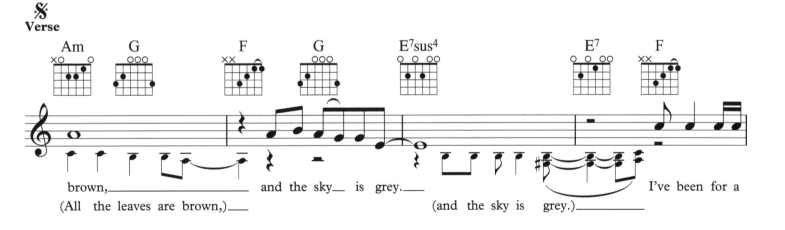

brown,_____ and the sky__ is grey.__

(All the leaves are brown,)__ (and the sky is grey.)____ I've been for a

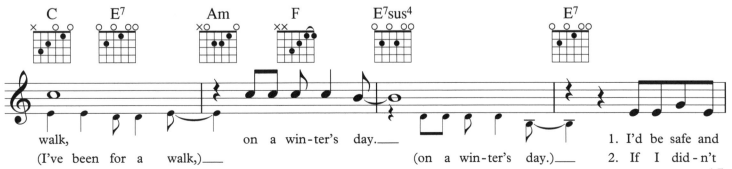

walk, on a win-ter's day.__

(I've been for a walk,)__ (on a win-ter's day.)__ 1. I'd be safe and
2. If I did-n't

The Cave

Words & Music by Mumford & Sons

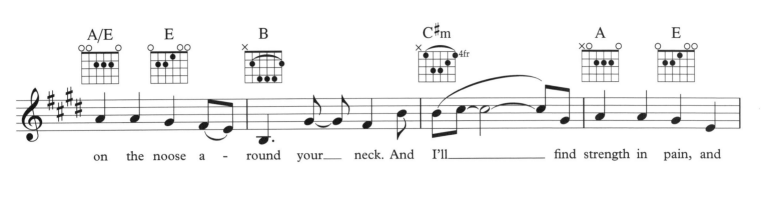

on   the   noose a - round   your___   neck. And   I'll_____ find   strength   in   pain,   and

To Coda ⊕

I_____ will   change   my___   ways.   I'll   know   my___   name   as   it's   called   a - gain.

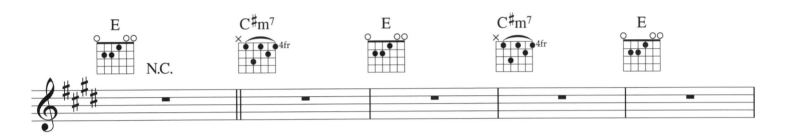

N.C.

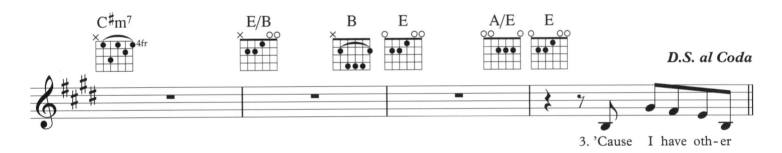

D.S. al Coda

3. 'Cause   I   have   oth- er

Verse

⊕ *Coda*

5. So   come   out   of   your   cave   walk- ing   on   your

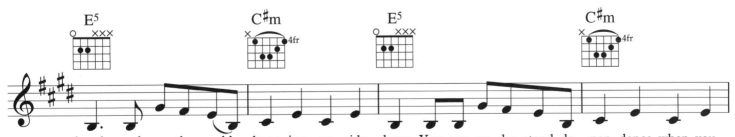

hands,   and   see   the   world___   hang- ing   up- side   down.   You   can   un- der- stand   de - pen- dence   when   you

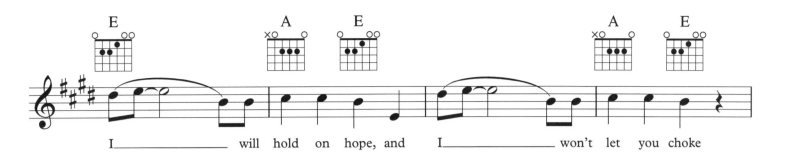

I_____ will hold on hope, and I_____ won't let you choke

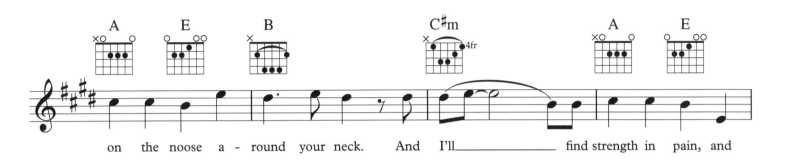

on the noose a - round your neck. And I'll_____ find strength in pain, and

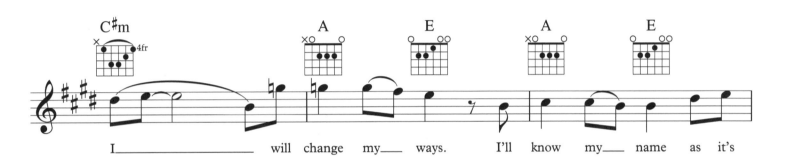

I_____ will change my__ ways. I'll know my__ name as it's

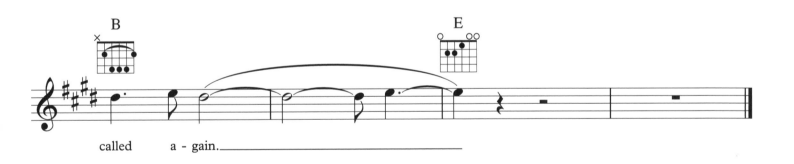

called a - gain._____

Verse 2
The harvest left no food for you to eat,
You cannibal, you meat-eater, you see.
But I have seen the same,
I know the shame in your defeat.

Verse 3
'Cause I have other things to fill my time,
You take what is yours and I'll take mine.
Now let me at the truth,
Which will refresh my broken mind.

Verse 4
So tie me to a post and block my ears,
I can see widows and orphans through my tears.
And know my call despite my faults
And despite my growing fears.

Chasing Pavements

Words & Music by Adele Adkins & Eg White

Arpeggio style:

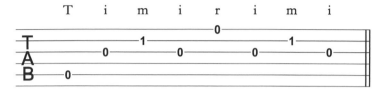

> Try this picking pattern throughout the intro and first verse; then switch to a simple strumming pattern for contrast.

Capo: Fret 3

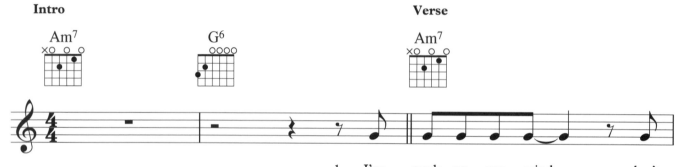

1. I've made up my mind,— don't

need to think it o-ver. If I'm wrong I am— right,— don't need to look no fur-ther. This ain't

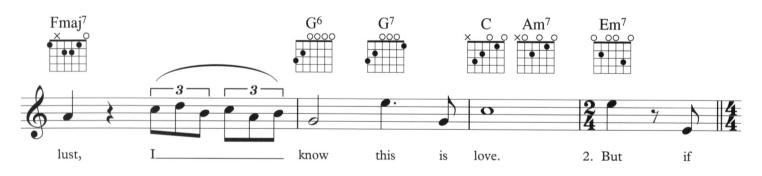

lust, I_____ know this is love. 2. But if

(2.) I tell the world, I'll nev-er say e-nough, 'cause it was not said to— you, and that's ex-
(3.) build my-self up— and fly a-round in cir-cles, wait-ing as my heart drops and my

-act - ly what I need to do if I   end_____ up   with you.
back be - gins to tin - gle. Fin - al - ly,   could_____ this__ be   it or

% Chorus

Should I give up?   Or should I   just keep chas-ing pave-ments   e - ven if it leads no - where?___

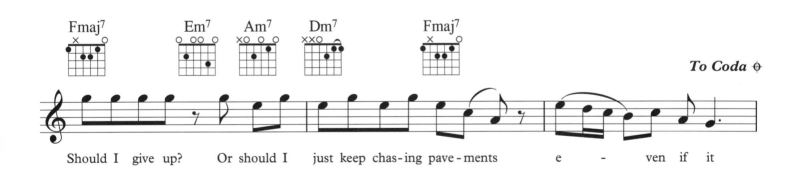

___ Or would it be a waste   e - ven if I knew my place? Should I leave it there?

To Coda ⊕

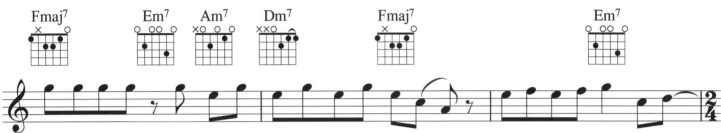

Should I give up?   Or should I   just keep chas-ing pave - ments   e - ven if it

1.   **2.**

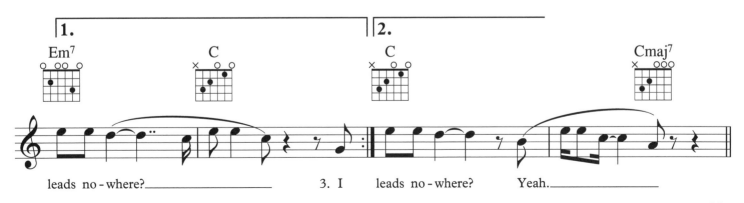

leads no - where?_____   3. I leads no - where? Yeah._____

Bridge

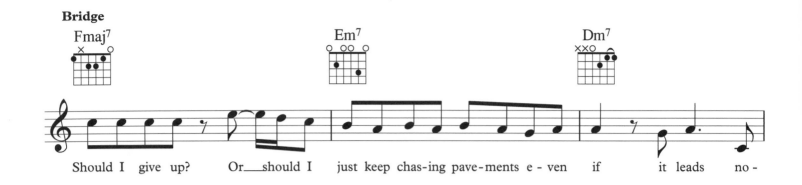

Should I give up? Or___should I just keep chas-ing pave-ments e - ven if it leads no-

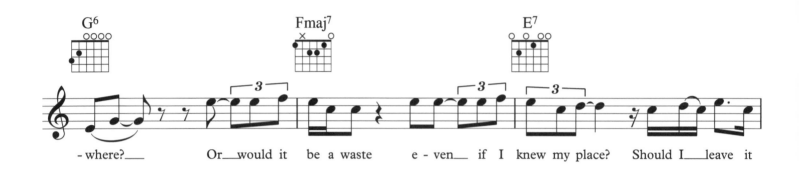

- where?___ Or___would it be a waste e - ven___ if I knew my place? Should I___leave it

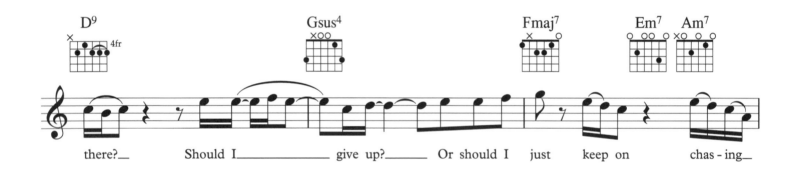

there?___ Should I_____ give up?_____ Or should I just keep on chas-ing___

D.S. al Coda

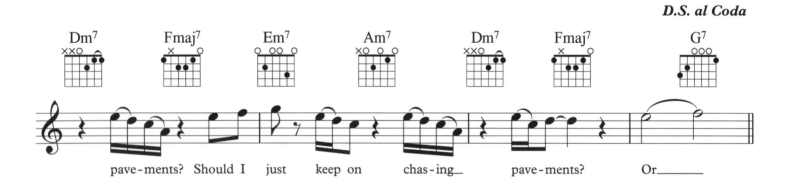

pave-ments? Should I just keep on chas-ing___ pave-ments? Or_____

Coda

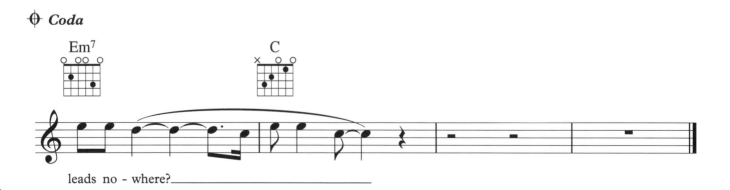

leads no - where?_____

24

Don't Know Why

Words & Music by Jesse Harris

Picking style:

don't know why____ I did - n't____ come.____

Verse

2. When I saw____ the break____ of day____
(Verse 3 & 4 see block lyric)

I wished that I____ could fly____ a - way,____

'stead of kneel - ing in the sand,

catch - ing tear - drops in my____ hand.____ My

Chorus

heart is____ drenched____ in____ wine.____

Verse 3:
Out across the endless sea,
I will die in ecstasy.
But I'll be a bag of bones,
Driving down the road alone.

Chorus:
My heart is drenched in wine, etc.

Verse 4:
Something has to make you run,
I don't know why I didn't come.
I feel as empty as a drum,
I don't know why I didn't come,
I don't know why I didn't come,
I don't know why I didn't come.

Don't Panic

Words & Music by Guy Berryman, Chris Martin, Jon Buckland & Will Champion

Strumming style:

Experiment by emphasising certain strums for rhythmic interest. The most important strums are on the first beat and the '&' after beat 2.

Intro

Verse

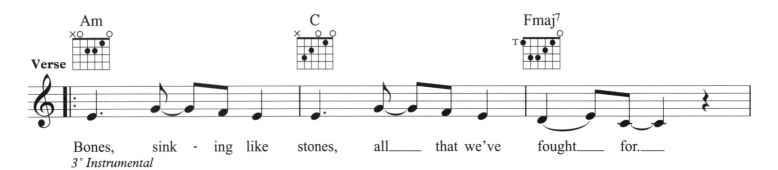

Bones, sink - ing like stones, all___ that we've fought___ for.___

3° Instrumental

Homes, plac - es we've grown, all___ of us are

Chorus

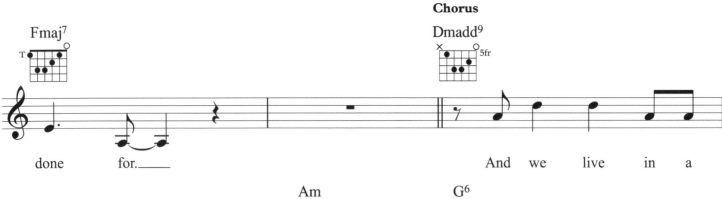

done for.___ And we live in a

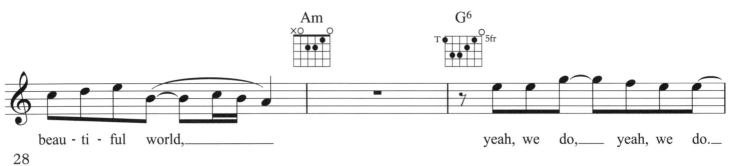

beau - ti - ful world,_____ yeah, we do,___ yeah, we do.___

Dmadd9

We live in a beau - ti - ful world._____

1, 2, 3. Fmaj7

4. Fmaj7

Guitar solo

Am   C   Fmaj7

Fmaj9   Am   C

Fmaj7   Am

Oh,   all___   that I

C   Fmaj7   Fmaj9

know, there's noth - ing here to run   from,___   'cause

Am   C   Fmaj7

yeah, ev - 'ry - bo - dy here's got some - bo - dy to lean   on.___

Dream Catch Me

Words & Music by Crispin Hunt, Gordon Mills & Newton Faulkner

Strumming style:

Capo: Fret 7

Bridge

See you as a moun-tain, a foun-tain, a God.___ See you as a des-

-cant soul___ in the set-ting sun. You as a sound,___ just as si-lent as none,___

___ I'm___ yours.___ There's a place I go___ when I'm a-lone,___

___ do an-y-thing I want,___ be an-y-one I wan-na be. But it is us___

D.S. al Coda

___ I see___ and I___ can-not___ be-lieve___ I'm___ fall-in'.

or else I won't___ come back at all.___

Every Rose Has Its Thorn

Words & Music by Bret Michaels, Bruce Johannesson, Robert Kuykendall & Richard Ream

Strumming style:

The strumming is based on sixteenth-notes (four per beat). Leaving out certain strums, as shown, creates an interesting rhythm.

To match original recording, tune down one semitone.

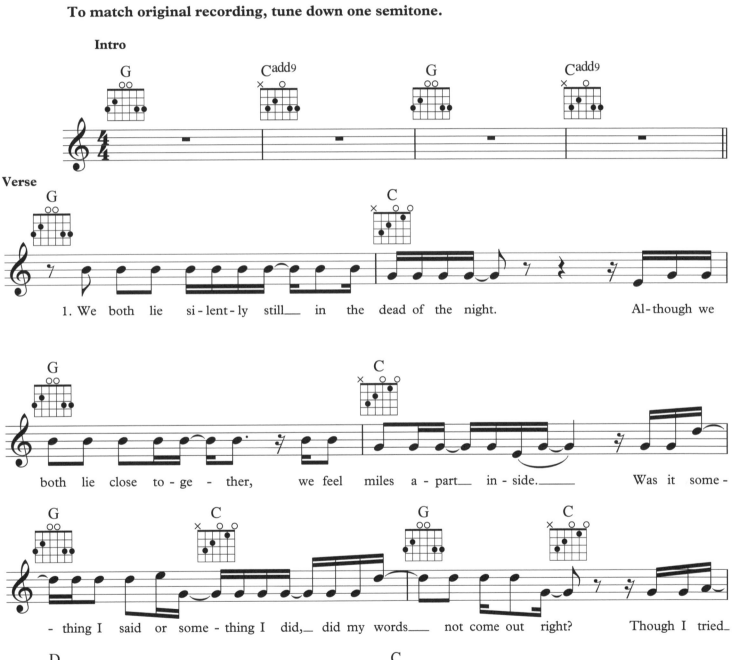

Chorus

- 'ry rose__ has its thorn,___ just like ev - 'ry night__ has its dawn,___

just like ev - 'ry cow - boy sings his sad,__

__ sad__ song:__ Ev - 'ry rose has its thorn.___ Yeah, it does.

2. I

Verse

lis - ten to our fav- 'rite song,__ play-ing on the ra - di - o,____ hear the D.-
3. I know I could have saved a love that night if I'd known what to say.

- J. say__ love's a game__ of ea - sy come and ea - sy go.____ But I won-
'Stead of ma - kin' love we both made our sep -'rate ways. And now I

- der, does he____ know? Has he ev - er felt__ like this?__ And I know__
hear you found some - bo - dy new and that I ne - ver meant that much to you. To hear__

Father And Son

Words & Music by Cat Stevens

Intro:

> In the intro, 'hammer on' to C/G: strum down on G on the 2nd beat, then change chord shape without strumming again.

To match original recording, tune down one semitone.

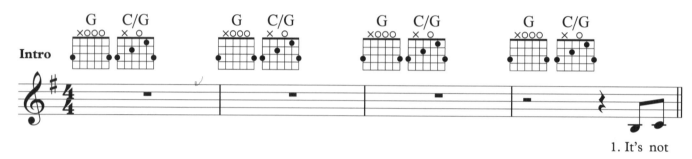

1. It's not

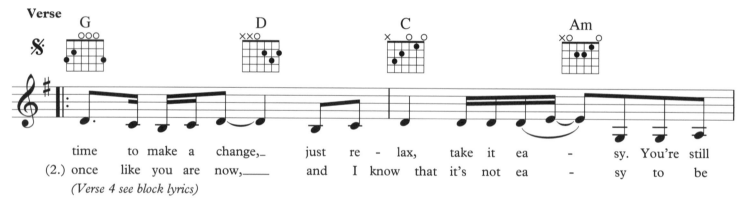

time to make a change,___ just re - lax, take it ea - sy. You're still
(2.) once like you are now,___ and I know that it's not ea - sy to be
(Verse 4 see block lyrics)

young, that's your fault,___ there's so much you have__ to know. Find__ a girl,
calm when you've found__ some - thing go ing on._____ But take your time,__

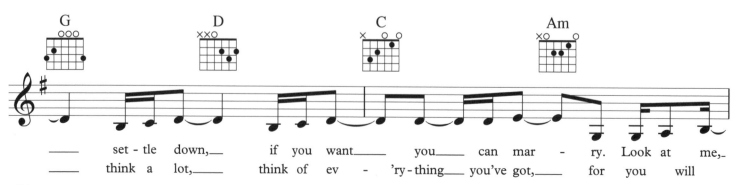

____ set - tle down,___ if you want___ you__ can mar - ry. Look at me,__
____ think a lot,___ think of ev - 'ry - thing__ you've got,___ for you will

36

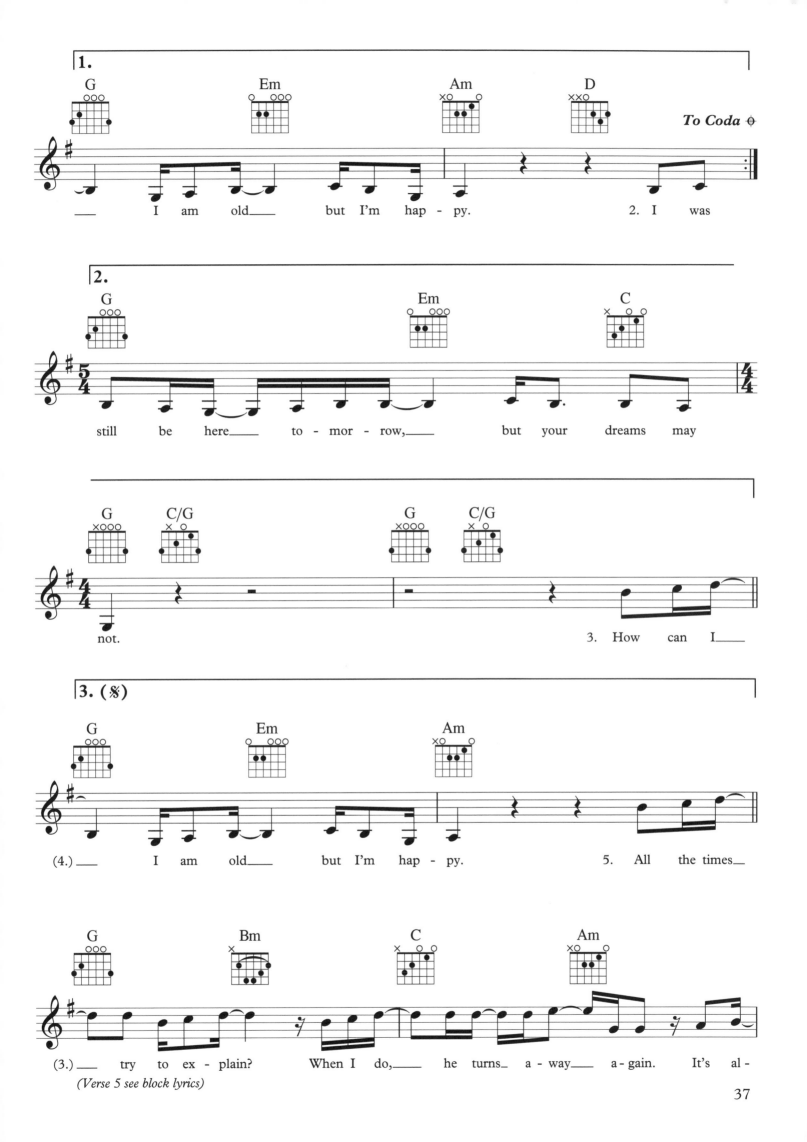

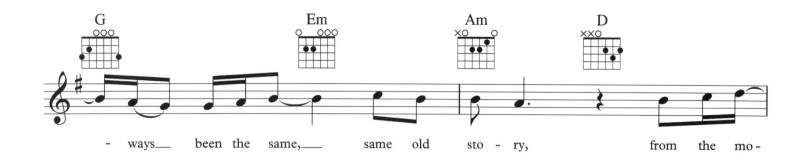

- ways___ been the same,___ same old sto - ry, from the mo -

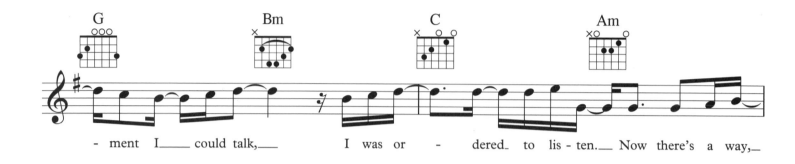

- ment I___ could talk,___ I was or - dered_ to lis - ten.___ Now there's a way,___

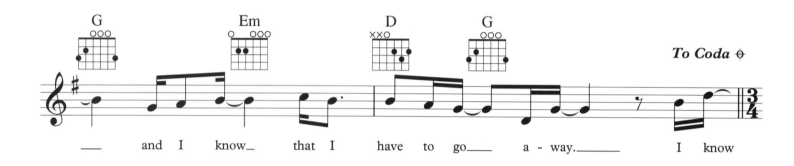

To Coda ⊕

___ and I know_ that I have to go___ a - way.___ I know

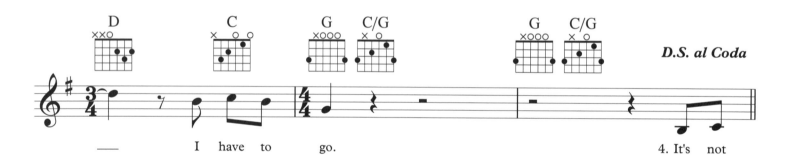

D.S. al Coda

___ I have to go. 4. It's not

⊕ *Coda*

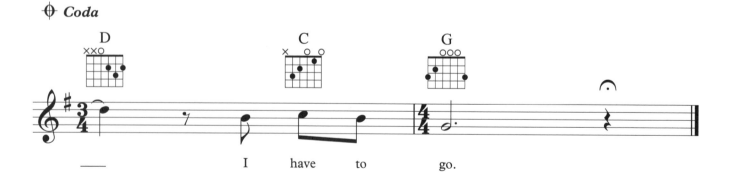

___ I have to go.

Verse 4:
It's not time to make a change,
Just sit down, take it slowly.
You're still young, that's your fault,
There's so much you have to go through.
Find a girl, settle down,
If you want you can marry.
Look at me, I am old but I am happy.

Verse 5:
And all the times that I've cried,
Keeping all the thing I knew inside,
It's hard, but it's harder to ignore it.
If they were right, I'd agree,
But it's them they know, not me,
Now there's a way,
And I know I have to go away.
I know I have to go.

Fields Of Gold

Words & Music by Sting

Picking style:

Intro

Bm¹¹

Play 7 times

Verse Bm⁷

You'll re - mem - ber me, when the
stay with me, will you

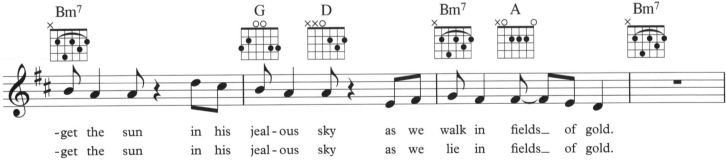

G   D

west wind moves_ up - on the fields_ of bar - ley. You'll for -
be my love_ a - mong the fields_ of bar - ley? We'll for -

Bm⁷   G   D   Bm⁷   A   Bm⁷

-get the sun in his jeal - ous sky as we walk in fields_ of gold.
-get the sun in his jeal - ous sky as we lie in fields_ of gold.

G   D   Bm⁷   G

So she took her love for to gaze a - while up-
See the west wind move like a lov - er so_ up-

39

Folsom Prison Blues

Words & Music by Johnny Cash

Strumming style:

Alternate the bass notes between the root note and the fifth of the chord: that's between the 6th & 5th strings for E.

(4.) bet there's rich folks eat - in' in a fan - cy din - ing car. They're
(6.) freed me from the pri - son, if that rail - road train was mine, I

prob - 'ly drink - in' cof - fee and smok - in' big cig - ars, but I
bet I'd move it on a little far - ther down the line,

knew I had it com - in', I know I can't be
far from Fol - som Pri - son, that's where I want to

free,_____ but those
stay,_____ And I'd

people keep a - mov - in', and that's what tor - tures____
let that lone - some whis - tle blow____ my blues____ a -

1. **2.** **3.**

me.____ 5. *Instrumental* 6. Well, if they
- way.____

43

Friday I'm In Love

Words by Robert Smith
Music by Robert Smith, Simon Gallup, Perry Bamonte, Porl Thompson & Boris Williams

Strumming style:

1 & 2 & 3 & 4 &

Capo: Fret 1

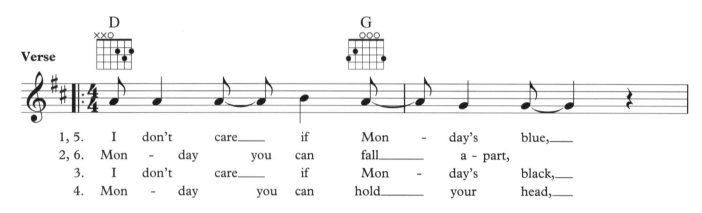

1, 5. I don't care___ if Mon - day's blue,___
2, 6. Mon - day you can fall___ a - part,
3. I don't care___ if Mon - day's black,___
4. Mon - day you can hold___ your head,___

Tues-day's grey___ and Wednes - day too.___ Thurs - day I don't care
Tues - day, Wednes-day break___ my heart.__ Oh, Thurs - day does n't ev -
Tues - day, Wednes-day heart___ at - tack.___ Thurs - day nev - er look -
Tues - day, Wednes-day stay___ in bed.__ Or Thurs - day watch the walls___

Fine

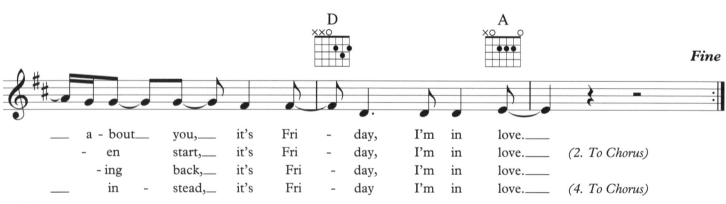

___ a - bout___ you,___ it's Fri - day, I'm in love.___
- en start,___ it's Fri - day, I'm in love.___ *(2. To Chorus)*
- ing back,___ it's Fri - day, I'm in love.___
___ in - stead,___ it's Fri - day I'm in love.___ *(4. To Chorus)*

Chorus

Sat - ur - day___ wait,___ 'cause Sun - day al - ways comes___

44

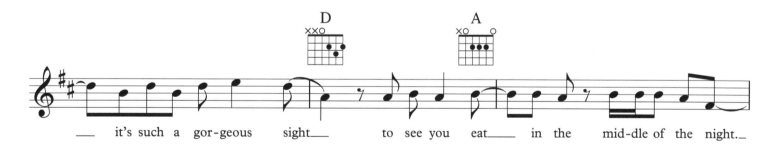

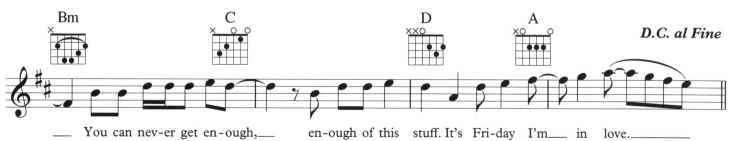

Fifty Ways To Leave Your Lover

Words & Music by Paul Simon

> Play sparsely-picked chords in the verse, before switching to a choppy up-tempo strumming style in the chorus.

Picking style:

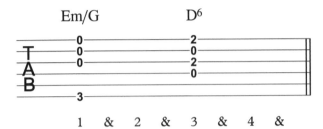

Strumming style:

Verse

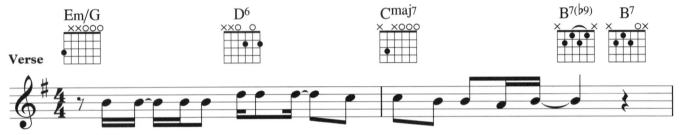

1. 'The prob - lem is all in - side_ your head', she said to me,_____
3. She said_ it grieves me so__ to see you in such pain, I wish there

the ans - wer is ea - sy if you take it lo - gic - 'lly_____
was some - thing I could do to make you smile a - gain.__ I said that

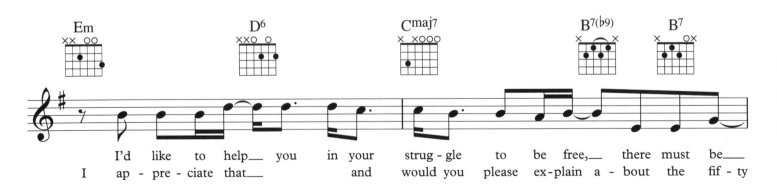

I'd like to help_ you in your strug - gle to be free,_ there must be__
I ap - pre - ciate that__ and would you please ex - plain a - bout the fif - ty

fif - ty ways___ to leave your lov - er._____

ways._____

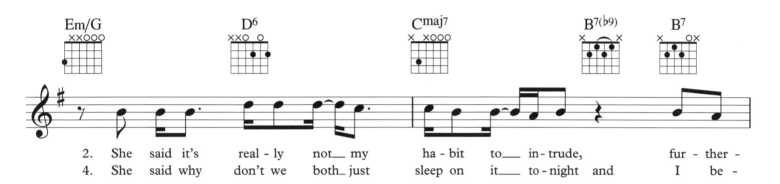

2. She said it's real - ly not___ my ha - bit to___ in - trude, fur - ther -

4. She said why don't we both___ just sleep on it___ to - night and I be -

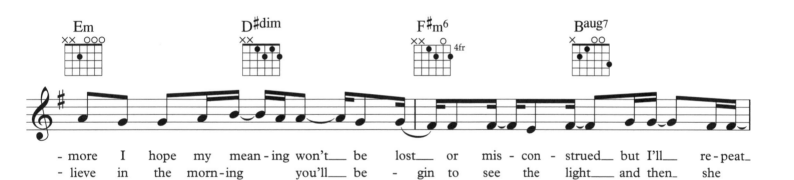

- more I hope my mean - ing won't___ be lost___ or mis - con - strued___ but I'll___ re - peat_

- lieve in the morn - ing you'll___ be - gin to see the light___ and then_ she

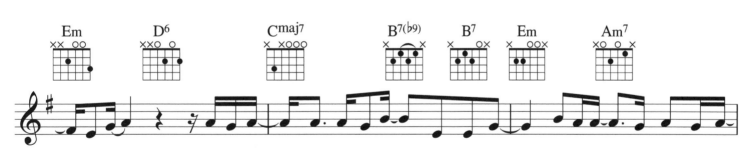

___ my - self_ at the risk___ of be - ing crude } there must be_____ fif - ty ways_ to leave your lov-

kissed me_ and I re - a - lized she pro - bab - ly was right,

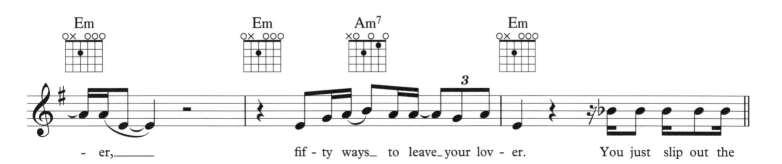

- er,_____ fif - ty ways_ to leave_ your lov - er. You just slip out the

Hallelujah

Words & Music by Leonard Cohen

Arpeggio style:

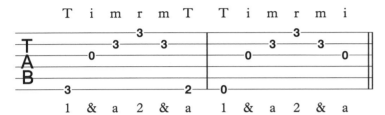

Focus on playing the picking pattern as precisely as possible. Let the notes of the chord ring out—this will really help the music flow.

Capo: Fret 5

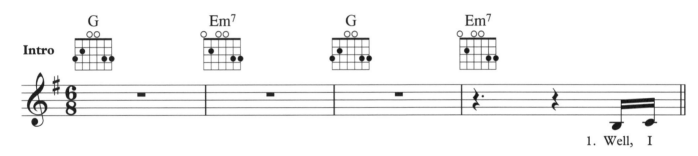

Intro

1. Well, I

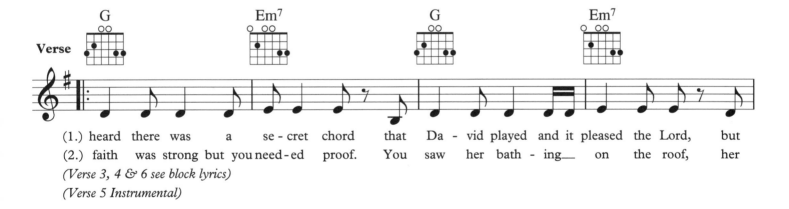

Verse

(1.) heard there was   a se - cret chord   that Da - vid played and it pleased the Lord,   but
(2.) faith   was strong but you need - ed   proof.   You   saw her bath - ing___ on   the roof,   her

(Verse 3, 4 & 6 see block lyrics)

(Verse 5 Instrumental)

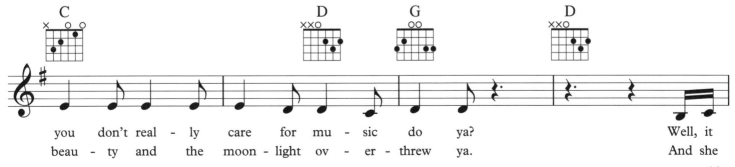

you don't real - ly   care   for mu - sic do ya?   Well, it
beau - ty and   the   moon - light ov - er - threw ya.   And she

49

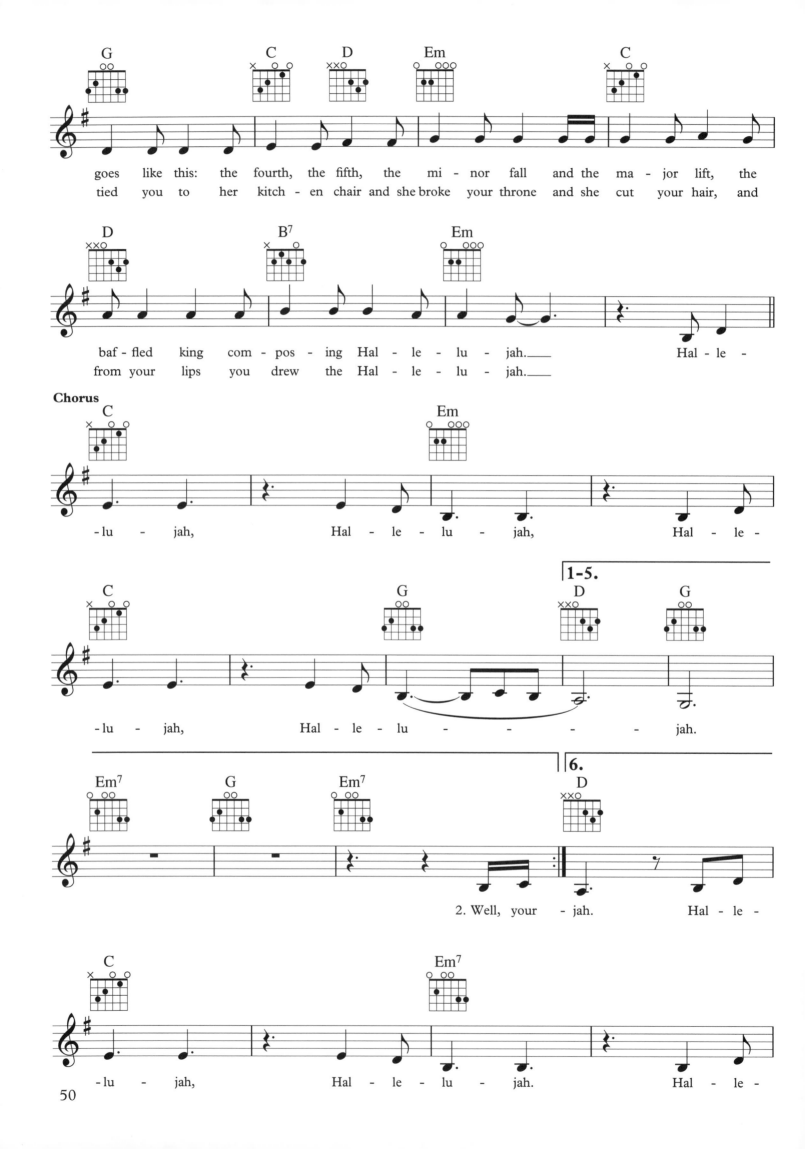

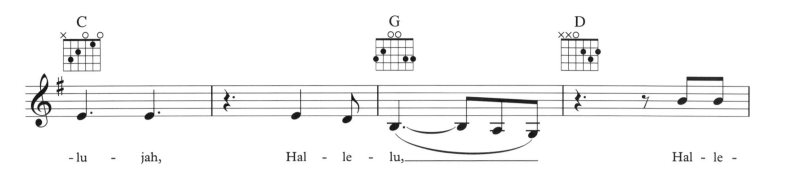

-lu - jah,   Hal - le - lu,_____   Hal - le -

-lu - jah.   Hal - le - lu - jah.___   Hal - le -

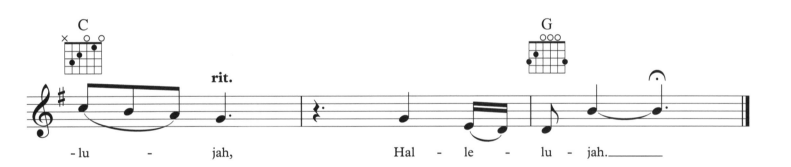

-lu - jah,   Hal - le - lu - jah._____

Verse 3:
Well, baby I've been here before
I've seen this room, and I've walked this floor,
You know, I used to live alone before I knew you.
And I've seen your flag on the marble arch
And love is not a victory march,
It's a cold and it's a broken Hallelujah.

Verse 4:
Well, there was a time when you let me know
What's really going on below,
But now you never show that to me do ya?
But remember when I moved in you
And the holy dove was moving too,
And every breath we drew was Hallelujah.

Verse 6:
Maybe there's a God above,
But all I've ever learned from love
Was how to shoot somebody who outdrew ya.
And it's not a cry that you hear at night,
It's not somebody who's seen the light,
It's a cold and it's a broken Hallelujah.

Hey, Soul Sister

Words & Music by Espen Lind, Pat Monahan & Amund Bjorklund

Strum in straightforward eighth-notes, with a heavy emphasis on the beats 2 & 4: the so-called *backbeat*, to add dynamics.

Strumming style:

Intro

Hey,___ hey,_____ hey.___ 1. Your

Verse

lip-stick stains on the front lobe of my left side brains. I knew I would-n't for-
2. Just in time, I'm so glad you have a one track mind like me. You gave_my life_ di-

- get you and so I went and let you blow my mind.___ Your
rec-tion, a game show love con-nec-tion we can't de-ny.___ I'm

sweet moon-beam, the smell of you in ev-'ry sin-gle dream I_ dream._
so ob-sessed. My heart is bound to beat right out my un-trimmed chest.

___ I knew when we col-li-ded you're the one I have de-
___ I be-lieve in you,___ like a vir-gin, you're Ma-

- ci - ded who's one of my kind.
- don - na. And I'm al-ways gon - na wan-na blow your mind.

Chorus

Hey soul sis - ter, ain't that Mis-ter Mis-ter on the ra - di - o, ste - re - o? The way

To Coda

you move ain't fair you know. Hey soul sis - ter, I don't wan-na miss a sin-gle

1.

thing you do to - night. Hey,

hey, hey.

2.

The way you can cut a rug. Watch-ing you is the on - ly drug I

53

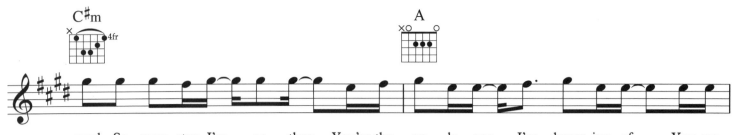

need. So gang-ster, I'm___ so thug.__ You're the on - ly one___ I'm dream-ing of.___ You see

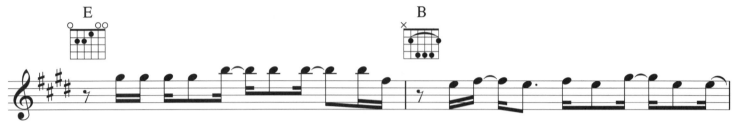

I can be my - self___ now fi - nal-ly. In fact___there's noth-ing I___ can't be.___

D.S. al Coda

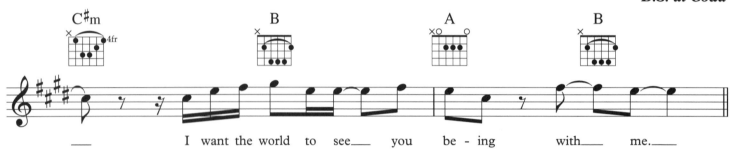

___ I want the world to see___ you be - ing with___ me.___

thing you do___ to - night._____ Hey soul sis - ter, I_____don't wan-na miss a sin-gle

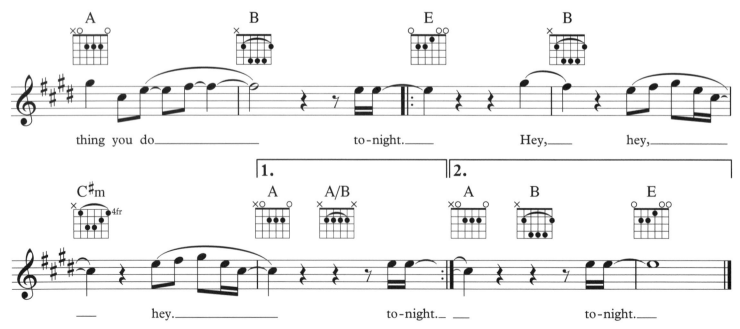

thing you do_____ to-night.___ Hey,___ hey,_____

1. to-night.__ __

2. to-night.___

___ hey._____

Ho Hey

Words & Music by Jeremy Fraites & Wesley Schultz

Strumming style:

Play this sparse pattern, but keep the strumming hand moving in sixteenth-notes, adding extra strums for the chorus.

Intro

Ho!   Hey!

Verse

(Ho!) 1. I've been try'n' to do__ it right.   (Hey!) I've been liv-ing a lone - ly life._____
(Ho!) 2. So   show me fa - mi - ly.   (Hey!) All the blood that I____would bleed._____
(Ho!) 3. I don't think you're right_ for him.   (Hey!) Look at what it might have been_ if you

(Ho!) I've been sleep - ing here_ in - stead.   (Hey!) I've been sleep - ing in__ my bed._____
(Ho!) I don't know where I____ be - long.   (Hey!) I don't know where I____went wrong._____
(Ho!) took a bus to Chi - na - town.   (Hey!) I'd be stand - ing on__ Ca - nal_____

To Coda ⊕   **1.**

(Ho!) I've been sleep-ing in__my bed._____   Hey!   Ho!
(Ho!) But I can write a song._____
(Ho!)   And Bo - we - ry._____

(Hey! Two, three...) I be-long with you, you be-long with me you're my___ sweet-

- heart.___ I be-long with you, you be-long with me you're my___ sweet...

D.S. al Coda

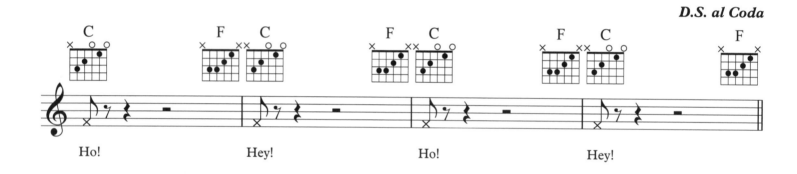

Ho! Hey! Ho! Hey!

Coda

(Hey!) (Ho!) And she'd be stand-ing next___ to me._____

Chorus

(Hey! Two, three...) I be-long with you, you be-long with me you're my___ sweet-

heart___   I be-long with you,   you be-long with me you're my___ sweet-

Bridge

heart.   And love,   we need___ it now.   Let's hope___

___   for some.   'Cause oh,___   we're

Chorus

bleed - ing out.   I be-long with you,   you be-long with me you're my___ sweet-

heart.___   I be-long with you,   you be-long with me you're my___ sweet...

Ho!   Hey!   Ho!   Hey!

Imagine

Words & Music by John Lennon

Arpeggio style:

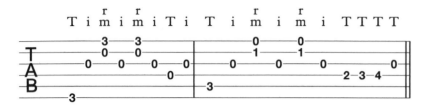

> The picking shown here is specific to the intro and verse, which alternate between G and C. Try simple strumming for the chorus.

Capo: Fret 5

Intro

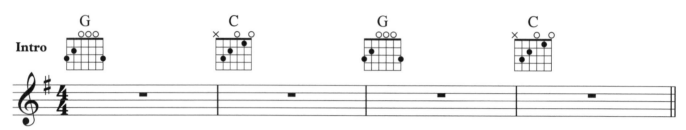

Verse

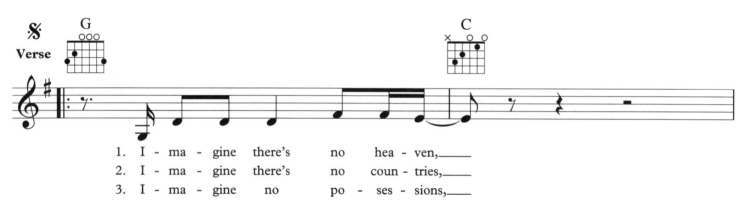

1. I - ma - gine there's no hea - ven,_____
2. I - ma - gine there's no coun - tries,_____
3. I - ma - gine no po - ses - sions,_____

it's ea - sy if you try._____
it is - n't hard to do._____
I won - der if you can._____

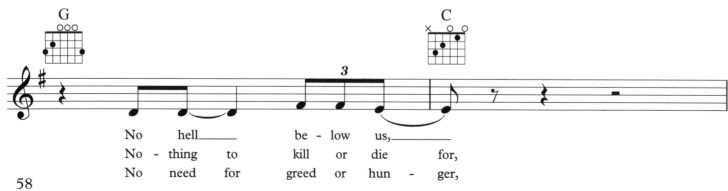

No hell_____ be - low us,_____
No - thing to kill or die for,
No need for greed or hun - ger,

Homeward Bound

Words & Music by Paul Simon

Strumming style:

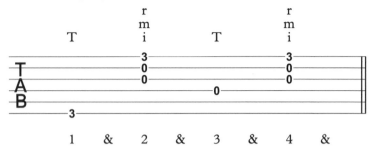

> The strumming for this song is extremely simple, so it needs to be accurate to provide a rock-solid beat and convincing feel.

Capo: Fret 3

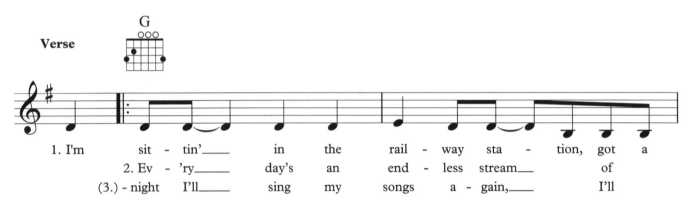

Verse

1. I'm sit - tin'_____ in the rail - way sta - tion, got a
2. Ev - 'ry_____ day's an end - less stream_____ of
(3.) - night I'll_____ sing my songs a - gain,_____ I'll

tick - et_____ for my des - tin - a - tion._____
cig - a - rettes and mag - a - zines._____
play the_____ game and pre - tend._____

Mm._____
Mm._____
Mm._____

On a tour_____ of one - night stands, my
And each town looks_____ the same to me, the
But all my words_____ come back to me in

F

suit - case   and   gui - tar_____   in hand,_____   and
mov - ies   and   the   fac - tor - ies,_____   and
shades   of   me - di - oc - rit - y,_____   like

G

ev - 'ry_____   stop   is   neat - ly   planned_____   for a
ev - 'ry_____   strang - er's   face   I   see_____   re -
emp - ti - ness   in   har - mon - y,_____   I

D(add4)

po - et_____   and   a   one_____   man_____   band._____
- minds   me_____   that   I   long_____   to_____   be..._____
need   some - one   to   com - fort_____   me._____

Chorus

G

___   Home - - ward_____
___
___

C   G

bound,   I   wish   I   was,_____

61

home - ward_____ bound.

Home, where my thought's____ es - ca - ping,

home, where my mu - sic's play - ing,

home, where my love____ lies wait - ing si - lent - ly

1, 2.

for me._____

3. To -

3.

G/F#   G/F   G

Si - lent - ly for me._____

I Will Wait

Words & Music by Mumford & Sons

Strumming style:

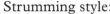

1 e & a 2 e & a 3 e & a 4 e & a

Capo: Fret 1

Intro Am   G/B   C   F(add9)   C/E   G

Verse C   F

1. And I came home_ like a stone and I fell
   dust_ which we've known will blow a-

C   G(sus4)   1.   2.

heav - y in - to your arms. These days of But
- way_____ with this new sun.

Pre-chorus Am   G/B   C   F(add9)   C/E   G

I'll_____ kneel down, wait for now._____ } And
I'll_____ kneel down, know my ground._____ }

Chorus C   Em   G(sus4)

I will_ wait, I will_ wait for you. And

I will wait, I will wait for you.

2. So break my step and relent. You for-
seen and him with less. Now in some

-gave and I won't forget. Know what we've 'Cause
way shake the excess.

Chorus

I will wait, I will wait for you. And

3. Now I'll be bold as well as strong and use my head

a-long-side my heart. So take my flesh and fix my

eyes, a teth-ered mind_____ free from the___ lies.

Bridge

I'll_____ kneel down, wait for now._____
I'll_____ kneel down, know my

ground._____

Raise_____ my____ hands,___
bow_____ my____ head,___

paint my spi - rit gold._____ And
keep my heart___ slow._____

'Cause

Play 4 times

I will_ wait, I will_ wait for you. (And)

65

The Joker

Words & Music by Steve Miller, Eddie Curtis & Ahmet Ertegun

The album version of this song is longer—and in a different key! This arrangement matches the single version.

Riff:

To match recording, tune down one semitone

Verse

1. Some peo-ple call me the space cow-boy. Yeah!—

(Verse 2: 8 bars instrumental)

3.   Peo-ple keep talk-ing a-bout me baby,

Some call me the gang-ster of love.—   Some peo-ple call me Mau-rice,

say I'm do-in' you wrong.—   But don't you wor-ry, don't wor-

— ry, no, don't wor-ry, Ma-ma,   cos I speak of the Pom-pa-tus of love.—

cos I'm right here at home.

(1.) Peo-ple talk a-bout me ba-by;   Say I'm do-in' you wrong, do-in' you

(2, 3.) You're the cu-test thing that I ev-er did see,   I love your peach — es, want to

(3º fade begins)

66

wrong._____ But don't you wor-ry, ba - by, don't wor - ry, cos I'm
shake your tree. Lovey dovey, lovey dovey, lovey dovey all the time.

right here, right here, right here, right here at home.___ Cos I'm a
Ooh - wee, baby, I should show you a good time.

Chorus

(𝄋) *Instrumental*

pick - er, I'm a grin - ner, I'm a lov - er, and I'm a sin - ner. I play my mu - sic in the

sun._____ I'm a jok - er, I'm a smok - er, I'm a mid - night tok - er.

1, 3.   *3° D.C. to fade* ‖**2.**   *D.S.*

{ I get my lov - ing on___ the run. Ooh._____ Ooh._____
{ I sure don't want to hurt no -   - one._____

Knockin' On Heaven's Door

Words & Music by Bob Dylan

Strumming style:

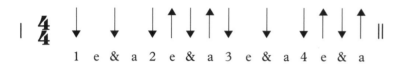

Keep the strumming hand moving in sixteenth-notes throughout, but play simple eighth-notes on beats 1 and 3.

Verse

1. Ma - ma, take__ this badge__ from me.____
(Verse 2 see block lyrics)

I can't use it a - ny - more.____

It's get - ting dark,____ too dark__ to see;____

I feel like I'm knock - in' on hea - ven's door.____

Chorus

Knock, knock, knock - in' on hea - ven's door.____

D.C. al Coda
To Coda ⊕

Knock, knock, knock - in' on hea - ven's door.____

⊕ *Coda*

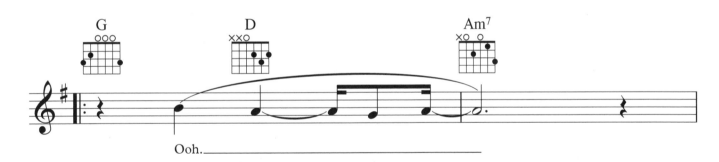

Ooh.____

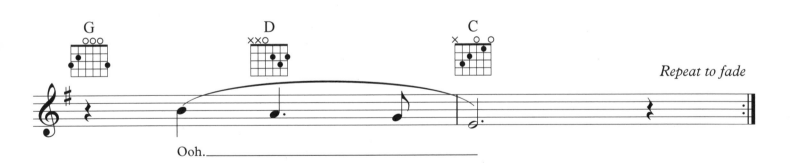

Repeat to fade

Ooh.____

Verse 2:
Mama, put my guns in the ground
I can't shoot them anymore
That long black cloud is comin' down
I feel like I'm knockin' on Heaven's door.

Jolene

Words & Music by Dolly Parton

Arpeggio style:

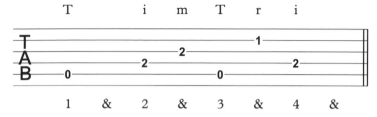

Practise the picking pattern on the A minor chord several times before trying it with the other chords.

Capo: Fret 4

G

please don't take him just be - cause___ you___ can.___

1. Your___

Verse
Am   **C**   **G**

(1.) beau - ty is___ be - yond___ com - pare,___ with flam - ing locks___ of au -
(2.) talks a - bout___ you in___ his sleep, and there's no - thing I___ can do___
3. You could have___ your choice___ of men, but I could nev - er love___

Am   **G**

- burn hair,___ with iv - 'ry skin___ and eyes of em - 'rald___
___ to keep___ from cry - ing when___ he calls your name, Jo -
___ a - gain.___ He's the on - ly one for me, Jo -

Am

green.___
- lene.___
- lene.___

Your___
And
I

C   **G**

smile is like a breath___ of spring, your voice___ is soft___ like
I can eas - 'ly un - der - stand how you___ could eas - 'ly
had to have this talk___ with you,___ my hap - pi - ness___ de -

Lay, Lady, Lay

Words & Music by Bob Dylan

Strumming style:

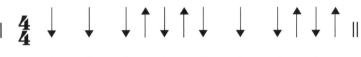

Intro

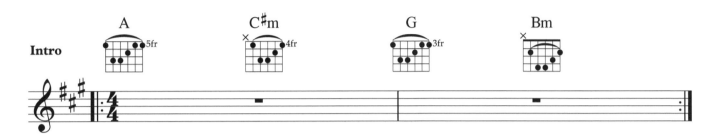

Chorus

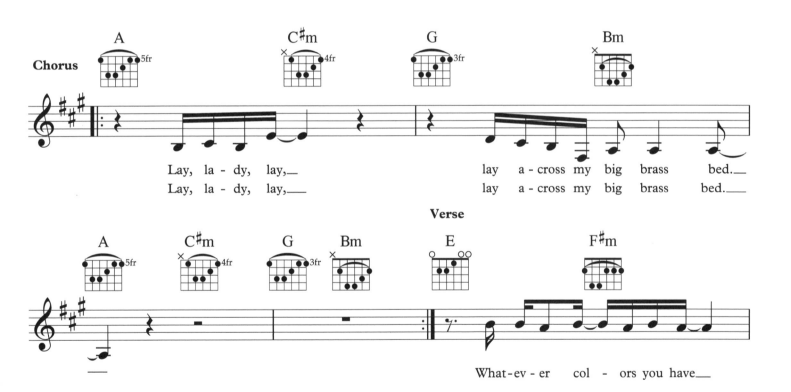

Lay, la - dy, lay,___ lay a - cross my big brass bed.___
Lay, la - dy, lay,___ lay a - cross my big brass bed.___

Verse

What - ev - er col - ors you have___

in your mind,_ I'll show them to you and you'll see them shine.

Let It Be

Words & Music by John Lennon & Paul McCartney

The fast-changing chord sequences emulate the original piano part. Simplify these by only playing the chords that occur on strong beats if you like.

1. When I

Verse

find my-self___ in times of trou-ble   Moth-er Ma - ry comes to me,

(Verses 2 & 3 see block lyrics)

speak-ing   words of wis - dom,   let it   be._____   And

in my   hour   of dark - ness   she is   stand-ing   right in front__ of me,___

speak-ing   words   of   wis - dom,   let   it   be._____   Let   it   be,___

Chorus

___ let   it   be,___ let   it   be,_____ let   it   be.____   Whis-per   words   of   wis - dom,   let   it   be.__
(2°, 3°) There   will   be__   an   an - swer,   let   it   be.__

1, 3.   **2.**

_____   2. And   when   _____   Let   it   be,__   let   it   be,__   let   it   be,__
_____

_____   let   it   be.__   Whis-per   words   of   wis - dom,   let   it   be._

Let it be,— let it be,— let it be,— let it be.— There will be— an ans-wer, let it be.—

Let it be,— let it be,— let it be,— let it be.—

Whis-per words of wis - dom, let it be.—

Verse 2:
And when the broken hearted people living in the world agree,
There will be an answer, let it be.
For though they may be parted, there is still a chance that they might see,
There will be an answer, let it be.

Let it be...

Verse 3:
And when the night is cloudy there is still a light that shines on me,
Shine until tomorrow, let it be.
I wake up to the sound of music, Mother Mary comes to me,
Speaking words of wisdom, let it be.

Life On Mars?

Words & Music by David Bowie

Strumming style:

It's a God-aw-ful small_ af - fair   to the girl with the mou-sy hair,
It's on A-me-ri-ca's tor-tured brow,   that Mick-ey mouse has grown up_ a cow,

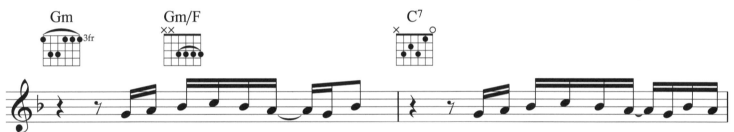

but her mum-my is yell - ing 'no',   and her dad - dy has told_ her to go.
now the work-ers have struck_ for fame,   cos Len-non's on sale_____ a-gain.

But her friend is no-where_ to be seen,   now she walks through her sunk - en dream
See the mice in their mil - lion hordes   from I - bi - za to the Nor - folk

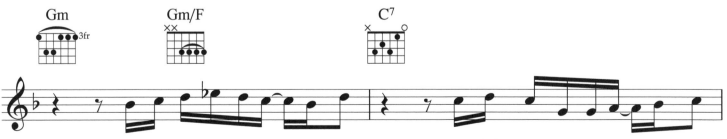

to the seat with the clear - est view,   and she's hooked to the sil - ver screen.
Broads,   Rule Bri-tan - nia is out_ of bounds   to my mo - ther, my dog_ and clowns.

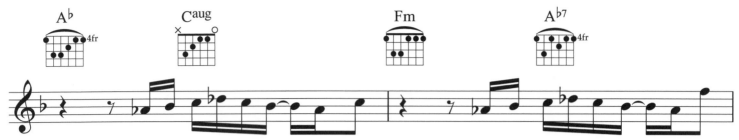

But the film is a sad - dening bore, for she's lived it ten times__ or more.
But the film is a sad - dening bore, 'cos I wrote it ten times or more,

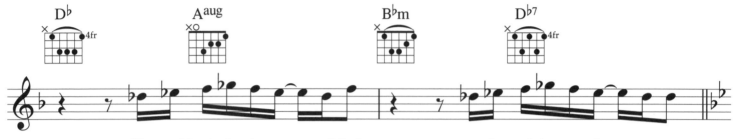

She could spit in the eyes__ of fools as they ask her to fo - cus on
it's a - bout to be writ__ a - gain as I ask her to fo - cus on

Chorus

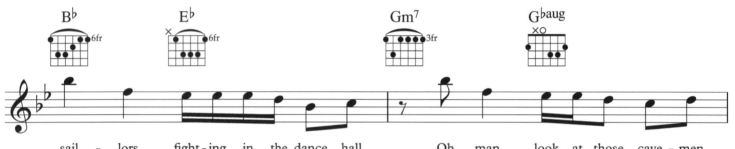

sail - lors fight - ing in the dance hall. Oh, man, look at those cave - men
sail - ors fight - ing in the dance hall. Oh, man, look at those cave - men

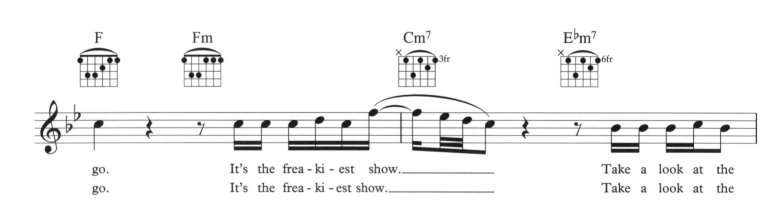

go. It's the frea - ki - est show._____ Take a look at the
go. It's the frea - ki - est show._____ Take a look at the

law - man beat - ing up the wrong guy. Oh, man, won - der if he'll ev - er know
law - man beat - ing up the wrong guy. Oh, man, won - der if he'll ev - er know

he's in the best sell-ing show._____ Is there life_ on Mars?_____

he's in the best sell-ing show._____ Is there life_ on Mars?_____

Love Story

Words & Music by Taylor Swift

Arpeggio style:

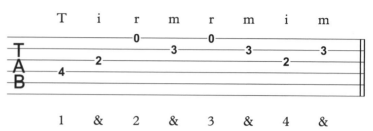

Intro

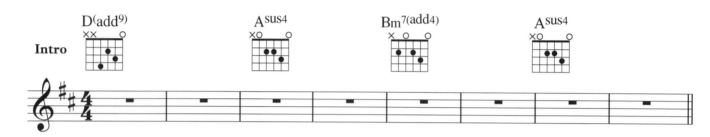

Verse

1. We were both young when I first saw___ you. I close my eyes___ and the

flash-back starts.__ I'm stand-in' there on a bal-co-ny in sum-mer air.

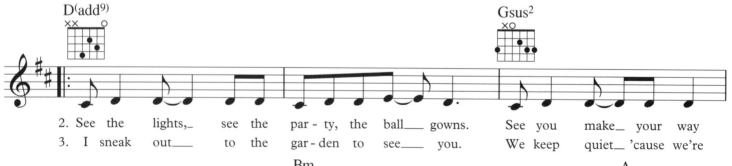

2. See the lights,__ see the par-ty, the ball___ gowns. See you make__ your way
3. I sneak out___ to the gar-den to see___ you. We keep quiet__ 'cause we're

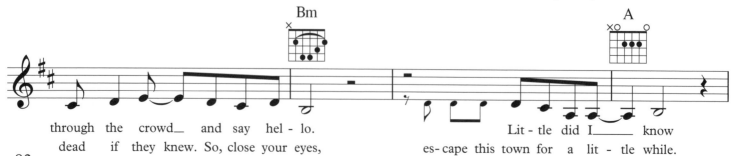

through the crowd__ and say hel-lo.   Lit-tle did I_____ know
dead if they knew. So, close your eyes,   es-cape this town for a lit-tle while.

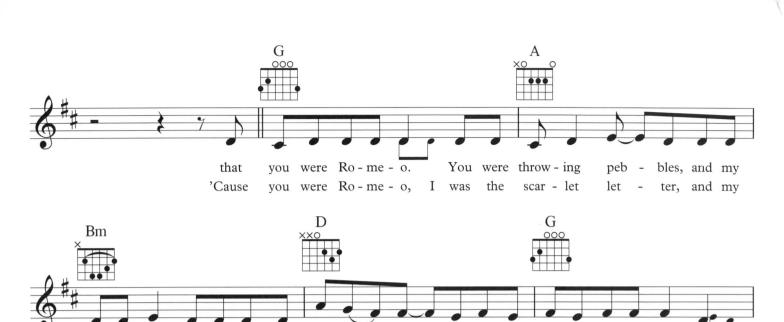

that you were Ro - me - o. You were throw - ing peb - bles, and my
'Cause you were Ro - me - o, I was the scar - let let - ter, and my

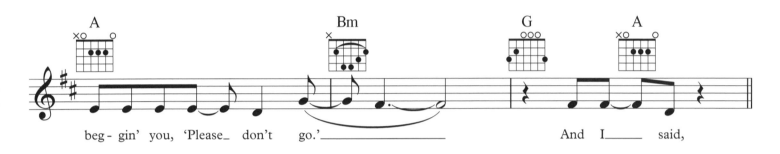

dad - dy said, 'Stay a - way from Ju - li - et.'___ And I was cry - in' on the stair - case,
dad - dy said, 'Stay a - way from Ju - li - et.'___ But you were ev - 'ry - thing to me. I was

beg - gin' you, 'Please_ don't go.'_____ And I_____ said,

Chorus

'Ro - me - o, take me some - where we can be a - lone. I'll be wait - ing.

All there's left to do is run. You'll be the prince and I'll be the prin - cess.

1.

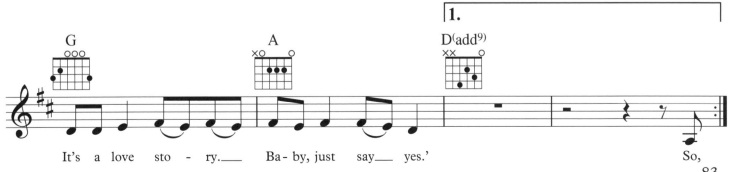

It's a love sto - ry.___ Ba - by, just say_ yes.' So,

Make You Feel My Love

Words & Music by Bob Dylan

Mrs. Robinson

Words & Music by Paul Simon

You can play the picked riff wherever you see the chord of **E**, or else use the strumming pattern throughout.

Ordinary World

Words & Music by John Taylor, Nick Rhodes, Simon Le Bon & Warren Cuccurullo

Strumming style:

1 e & a 2 e & a 3 e & a 4 e & a

Capo: Fret 4

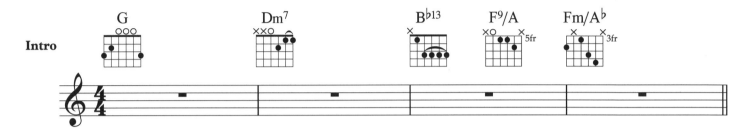

Intro

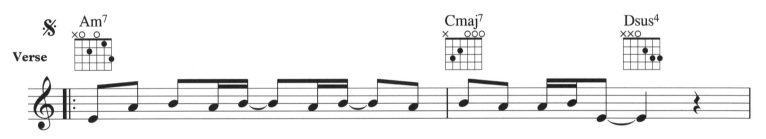

Verse

1. Came in from a rai - ny Thurs - day on the av - e - nue,___
2. Pas - sion or co - in - ci - dence_ once prompt - ed you to say,___
3. Pa - pers in the road - side tell___ of suf - fer - ing and greed,___

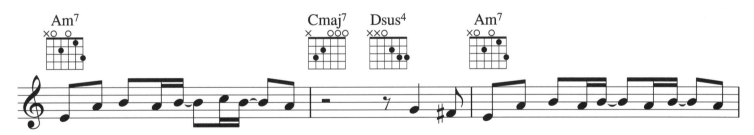

thought I heard you talk - ing soft - ly.   I turned on the lights, the T. - V.
'Pride will tear us both a - part.'___   Well, now pride's gone out the win - dow cross the
here to - day, for got___ to mor - row,   Ooh,___ here be - sides the news of ho - ly

To Coda ⊕

and the rad - i - o,___   still I can't es - cape_ the ghost of___ you.___
roof-top run a - way,___   left me in the vac - uum of___ my - heart.___
war and ho - ly need,___   ours is just a lit - tle sor - rowed_ talk.

Am⁷   Em

What has happ-ened to____ it all?____ 'Cra-zy', some would say.____
What is happ-'ning to____ me?____ 'Cra-zy', some would say.____

B⁷   Cmaj⁷

Where is the life____ that I re-cog-nize? (Gone a-way.)
Where is my friend____ when I need you most? (Gone a-way.)

Chorus

G   Dm⁷

But I won't cry for yes-ter-day,____ there's an or - di-nar - y

B♭   Am⁷   C(add2)   G

world, some-how I have to find.____ And as I try to make my way,_

Dm⁷   B♭   Am⁷

____ to the or - di-nar - ry world, I will learn to sur-vive.__

1.   **2.**

A♭   Am⁷ Am⁶ Am⁷   D   C(add2)

Redemption Song

Words & Music by Bob Marley

Strumming style:

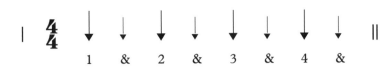

Strum in even eighth-notes, accenting the first strum of each beat and 'ghosting' the others—then experiment with accents for some lively alterations.

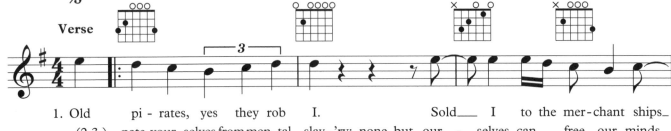

1. Old pi - rates, yes they rob I. Sold___ I to the mer - chant ships___
(2,3.) - pate your-selves from men-tal slav -'ry; none but our - selves can free our minds.__

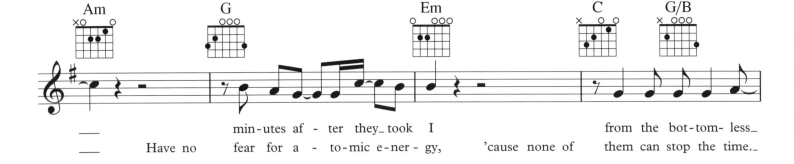

___ min - utes af - ter they_ took I from the bot-tom- less__
___ Have no fear for a - to-mic e-ner - gy, 'cause none of them can stop the time.__

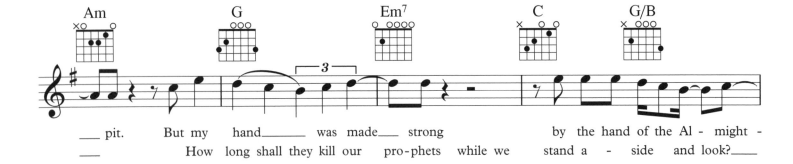

___ pit. But my hand_____ was made__ strong by the hand of the Al - might -
___ How long shall they kill our pro-phets while we stand a - side and look?___

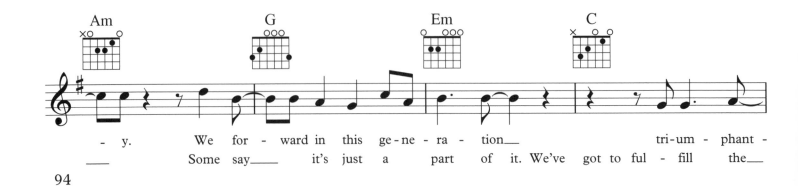

- y. We for - ward in this ge - ne - ra - tion___ tri - um - phant___
___ Some say___ it's just a part of it. We've got to ful - fill the___

94

95

Rocket Man

Words & Music by Elton John & Bernie Taupin

Strumming style:

Verse

1. She packed__ my bags__ last night pre - flight:_____
2. Mars ain't the kind__ of place__ to raise your kids;__

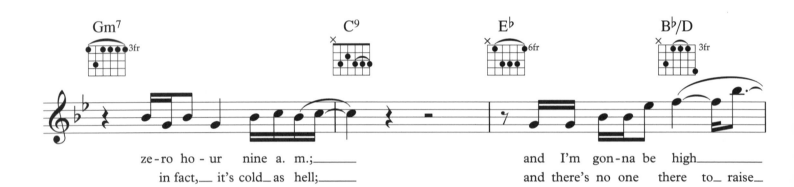

ze-ro ho - ur nine a. m.;_____ and I'm gon-na be high__
in fact,__ it's cold__as hell;_____ and there's no one there to__ raise__

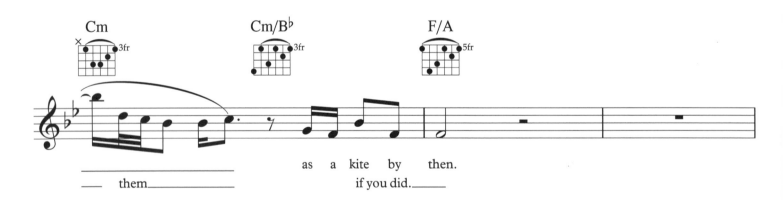

as a kite by then.
_____ them_____ if you did._____

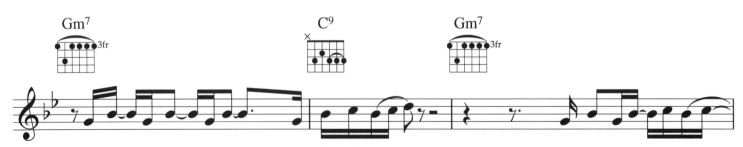

I miss__the Earth so much, I miss my wife;__ it's lone-ly out__ in space__
And all__ the science I don't un - der - stand:__ it just__my job__ five days a week.__

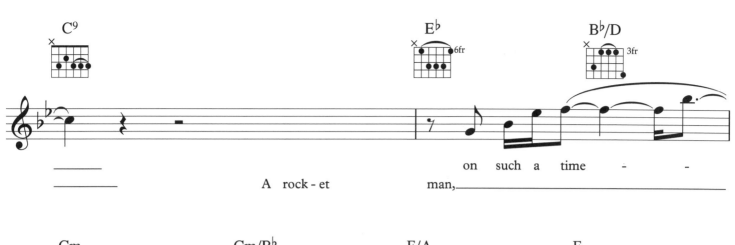

_____ on such a time - -

A rock - et man,_____

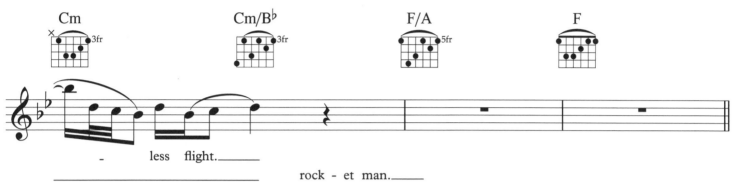

_ less flight._____

_____ rock - et man._____

Chorus

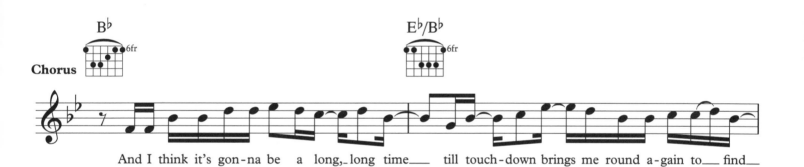

And I think it's gon-na be a long,_long time_____ till touch-down brings me round a-gain to_____ find

_____ I'm not the man_ they think I am at home,_____ oh, no,_____ no,_____ no._____ I'm a

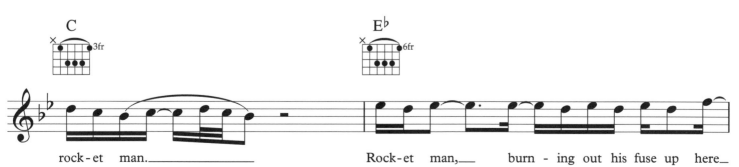

rock - et man._____

Rock-et man,_____ burn - ing out his fuse up here_____

97

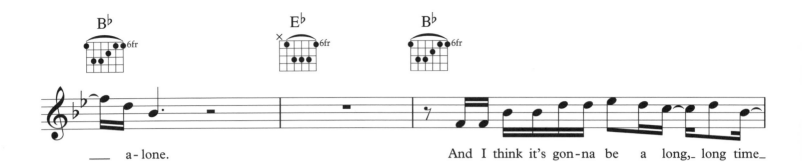

___ a-lone._   _And I think it's gon-na be a long,_ long time__

___ till touch-down brings me round a-gain to__ find__ I'm not the man_ they think I am at home,__

___ oh, no,__ no,__ no.__ I'm a rock-et man._____

To Coda ⊕

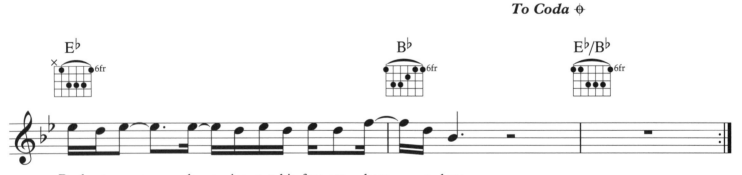

Rock-et man, burn-ing out his fuse up here__ a-lone._

⊕ **Coda**

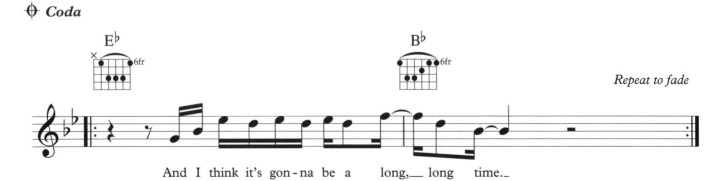

Repeat to fade

And I think it's gon-na be a long, long time.__

Romeo And Juliet

Words & Music by Mark Knopfler

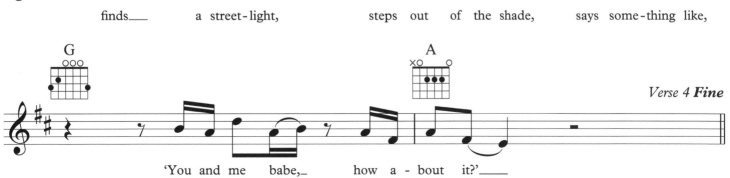

Capo: Fret 3

Intro

Verse

1, 4. A love-struck Ro-me-o
(Verses 2 & 3, see block lyrics)

sings a street-suss se-re-nade,—

lay-ing ev-'ry-bo-dy low—

with a love song that— he made,—

finds— a street-light,

steps out of the shade,

says some-thing like,

'You and me babe,— how a-bout it?'—

Verse 4 **Fine**

Ju - li - et says, 'Hey, it's Ro-me-o,   you near-ly gim-me a heart at- tack.'

He's un-der-neath the win-dow,   she's sing-ing   'Hey la,   my boy-friend's back,

you should-n't come a-round here,   sing-ing up at peo-ple like   that,

An - y - way,   what you gon-na do a - bout___ it?'_____ Ju - li -

Chorus

- et,   the dice were load - ed from___ the start,___ and I

(Chorus 2 & 3, see block lyrics)

bet,   and you ex - plod - ed in - to my heart and I for -

100

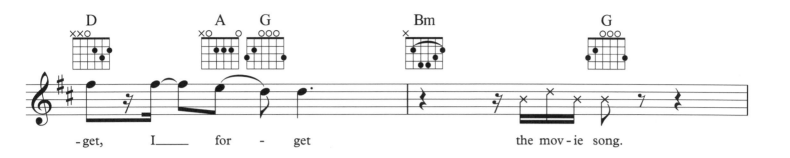

-get, I_____ for - get   the mov - ie song.

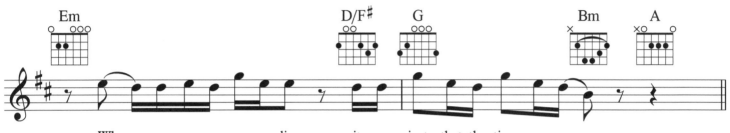

When_ you gon-na re - a - lise   it was just that the time was wrong,

D.S. al Fine

(3° play Link x 2)

Link

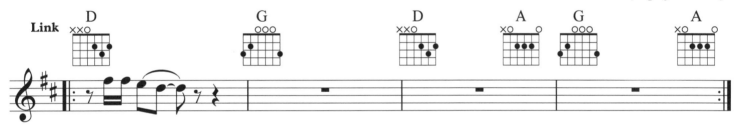

Ju - li - et?_____

Verse 2:
Come up on different streets
They both were streets of shame
Both dirty, both mean
Yes, and the dream was just the same
And I dreamed your dream for you
And now your dream is real
How can you look at me as if I was
Just another one of your deals?

Where you can fall for chains of silver
You can fall for chains of gold
You can fall for pretty strangers
And the promises they hold
You promised me everything
You promised me thick and thin, yeah
Now you just say 'Oh Romeo, yeah,
You know I used to have a scene with him'.

Chorus 2:
Juliet, when we made love you used to cry
You said, 'I love you like the stars above,
I'll love you till I die.'
There's a place for us, you know the movie song
When you gonna realise
It was just that the time was wrong, Juliet?

Verse 3:
I can't do the talk
Like they talk on the T.V.
And I can't do a love song
Like the way it's meant to be
I can't do everything
But I'd do anything for you
I can't do anything
Except be in love with you.

And all I do is miss you
And the way we used to be
All I do is keep the beat
And bad company
All I do is kiss you
Through the bars of a rhyme
Julie, I'd do the stars with you
Any time.

Chorus 3:
Juliet, when we made love you used to cry
You said, 'I love you like the stars above,
I'll love you till I die.'
There's a place for us, you know the movie song
When you gonna realise
It was just that the time was wrong, Juliet?

Save Tonight

Words & Music by Eagle-Eye Cherry

Strum in even eighth-notes, adding ghosted sixteenth-note strums where shown. This will create a more delicate and dynamic strumming rhythm.

Strumming style:

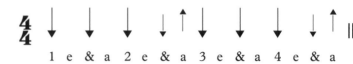

Do do do do   do do do do.   Do do do do   do do do do. 1. Go on and

Verse

close   the   cur tains   cos all we__ need   is can - dle   light,   you and__
(2.) log   on the   fi - re   and it__ burns   like me for   you. To - mor-row__

(Verse 3 instrumental)

__ me   and a bott-le of wine.   Gon-na hold you to-night.__   Well, we
__ comes   with one de - si - re____   to take me a-way, it's true.   It ain't
     3. To -

know   I'm go-ing a - way_ and how I____wish,   I wish it weren't__ so.   So take this
ea - sy   to say__good-bye,__ dar-ling,_please   don't__ start to cry____ cos
mor-row comes   to take me a - way._____ I wish that I,   that I could stay.

103

The Scientist

Words & Music by Guy Berryman, Chris Martin, Jon Buckland & Will Champion

Strumming style:

The strumming style for this song uses steady eighth-note strumming, with the on-beat strums accented—and all played with a down strum.

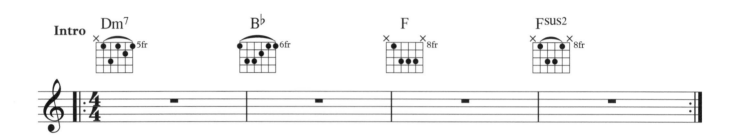

1. Come up to meet___ you, tell you I'm sor — ry, you don't know how love-
2. I was just gues — sing at num-bers and fig — ures, pull - ing the puz-

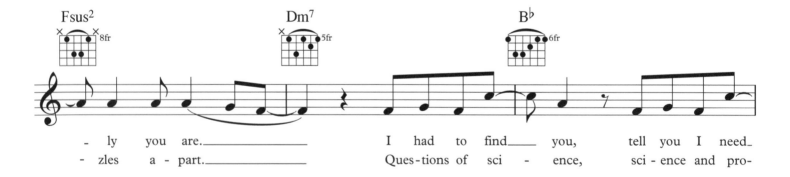

_ ly you are._____ I had to find___ you, tell you I need_
- zles a - part._____ Ques-tions of sci - ence, sci - ence and pro-

___ you, and tell you I'll set___ you a - part._____ Tell me your sec-
- gress that must speak as loud___ as my heart._____ Tell me you love_

Sing

Words & Music by Fran Healy

Strum simple eighth-notes, or else try this picking pattern, which emulates the original banjo part.

Arpeggio style:

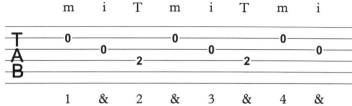

Capo: Fret 2

1. Ba - by, you've been go - in' so cra - zy, late - ly
2. Cold - er, cry - ing ov - er your shoul - der, hold

- ly no - thin' seems to be go - in' right. So
___ her, tell her ev - 'ry - thing's gon - na be fine. Sure -

___ a - lone, oh, why d'ya have to get so a - lone? You're
- ly you've been go - ing to hur - ry. Hur -

___ sore you've been wait - in' in the sun too long. But if you sing,
- ry, 'cause no - one's gon - na be stopped. Not if you sing,

Space Oddity

Words & Music by David Bowie

Strumming style:

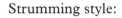
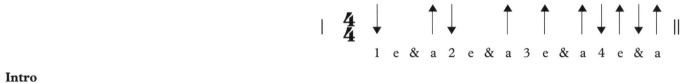

1 e & a 2 e & a 3 e & a 4 e & a

Intro

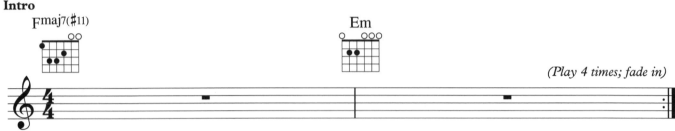

Fmaj7(♯11)   Em

(Play 4 times; fade in)

Verse

C   Em

Ground con-trol____ to Ma - jor Tom,____

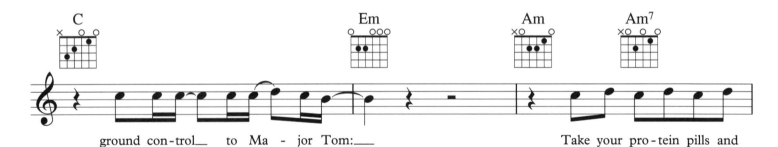

C   Em   Am   Am⁷

ground con-trol____ to Ma - jor Tom:____   Take your pro-tein pills and

D⁷   C   Em

put your hel-met on.____   Ground con-trol____ to Ma - jor Tom:____

Spoken: Ten,   *Nine,*   *Eight,*   *Seven,*

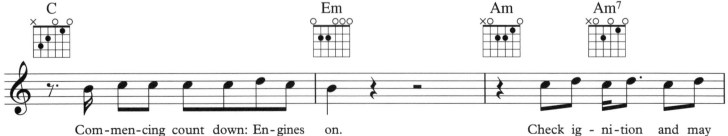

C   Em   Am   Am⁷

Com-men-cing count down: En-gines on.   Check ig - ni-tion and may

Six,   *Five,*   *Four,*   *Three,*   *Two,*   *One,*

Interlude

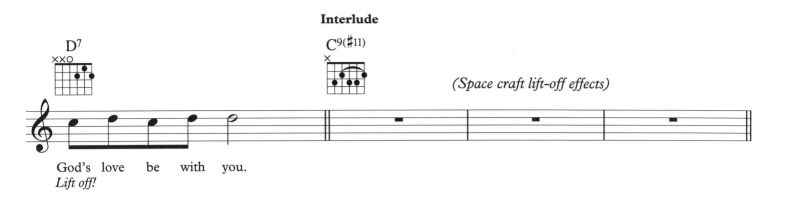

(Space craft lift-off effects)

God's love be with you.
Lift off!

Chorus

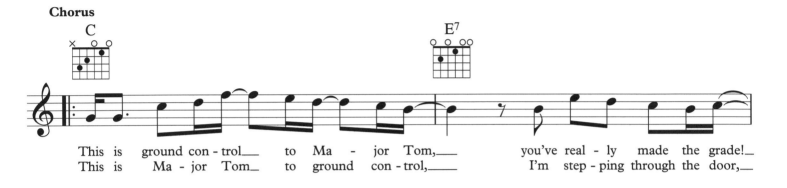

This is ground con - trol___ to Ma - jor Tom,___ you've real - ly made the grade!___
This is Ma - jor Tom___ to ground con - trol,___ I'm step - ping through the door,___

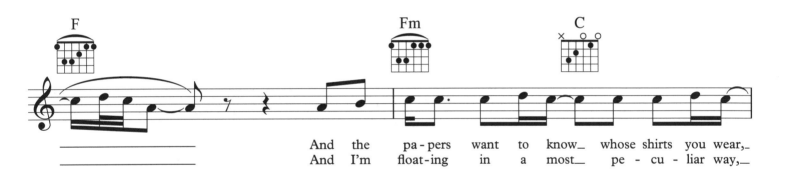

_____ And the pa - pers want to know__ whose shirts you wear,__
_____ And I'm float - ing in a most__ pe - cu - liar way,__

_____ Now it's time to leave the cap - sule if you dare.__
_____ And the stars look ve - ry dif - fe - rent to - day.__

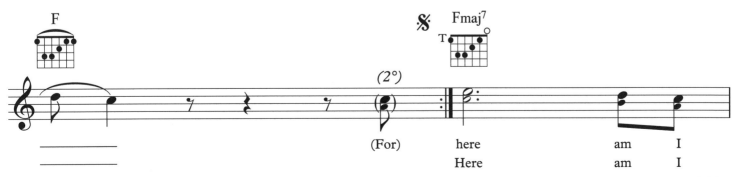

_____ (For) here am I
_____ Here am I

111

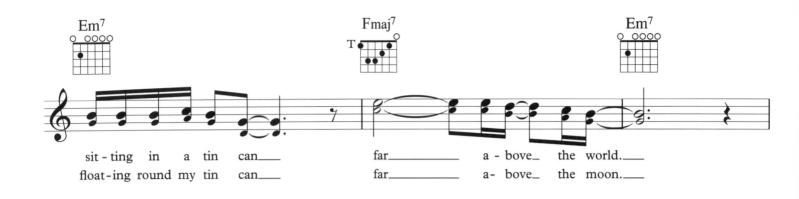

sit - ting in a tin can_____ far_____ a - bove_ the world._____
float-ing round my tin can_____ far_____ a- bove_ the moon._____

Pla - net Earth_ is blue and there's no-thing I can do.
Pla - net Earth_ is blue and there's no-thing I can do.

Bridge

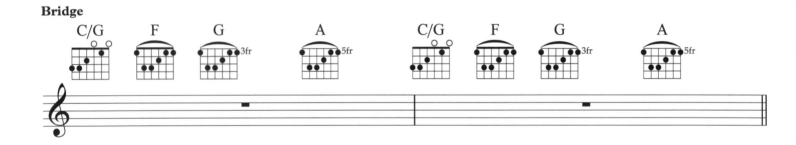

Guitar solo

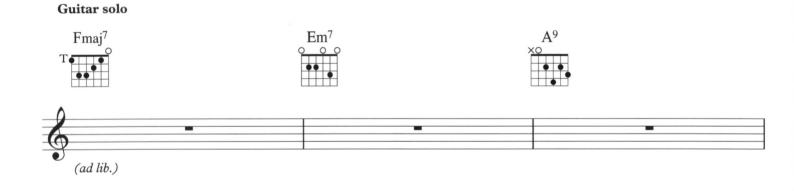

(ad lib.)

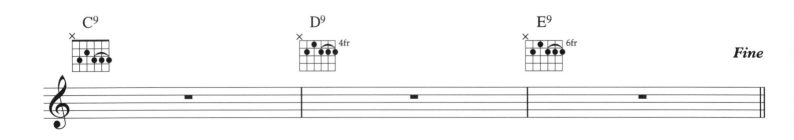

Fine

Though I'm past one hun-dred thou-sand miles_____ I'm feel-ing ve-ry still._

_____ And I think my space-ship knows which way to go,_____ tell my

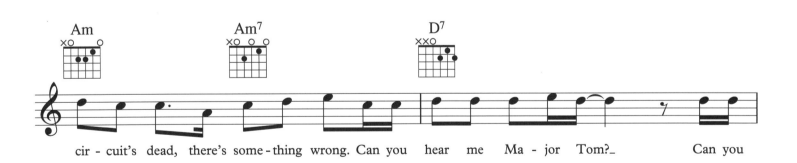

wife I love her ve-ry much, 'She knows.'_____ 'Ground con-trol to Ma-jor Tom: Your

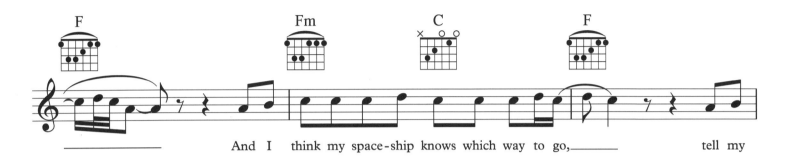

cir-cuit's dead, there's some-thing wrong. Can you hear me Ma-jor Tom?_ Can you

D.S. al Fine

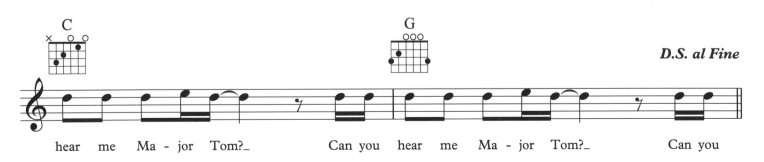

hear me Ma - jor Tom?_ Can you hear me Ma - jor Tom?_ Can you

113

Stand By Me

Words & Music by Ben E. King, Jerry Leiber & Mike Stoller

Strumming style:

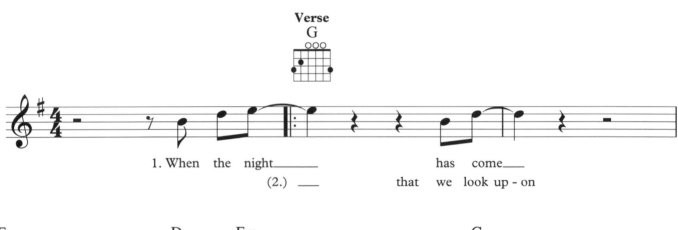

| Create a percussive 'slap' on beats 2 and 4 by bringing the strumming hand down hard onto the strings, providing a backbeat. |

Capo: Fret 2

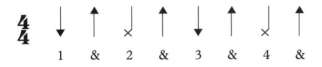

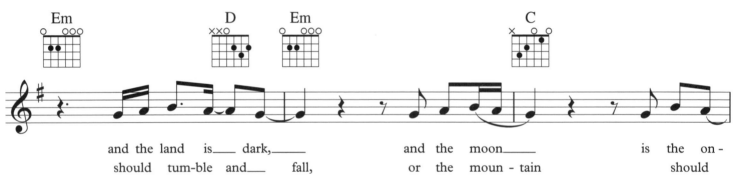

1. When the night＿＿＿ has come＿＿＿
(2.) ＿＿ that we look up-on

and the land is＿＿ dark,＿＿＿ and the moon＿＿＿ is the on-
should tum-ble and＿＿ fall, or the moun-tain should

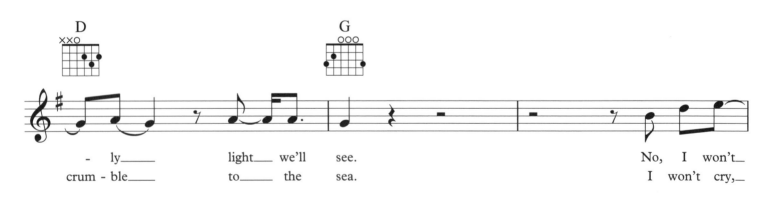

-ly＿＿ light＿＿ we'll see. No, I won't＿
crum-ble＿＿ to＿＿ the sea. I won't cry,＿

be a-fraid;＿＿＿ no, I＿＿＿
I won't cry;＿＿＿ no, I won't

The Sound Of Silence

Words & Music by Paul Simon

Picking style:

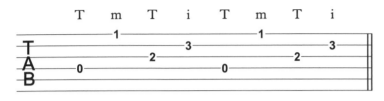

Capo: Fret 1

1. Hel - lo dark- ness, my old friend.
2. In rest - less dreams I walked a - lone
3. And in the nak - ed light I saw
4. 'Fools!' said I, 'You do not know

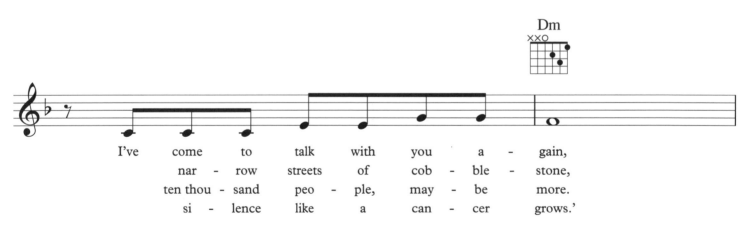

I've come to talk with you a - gain,
nar - row streets of cob - ble - stone,
ten thou - sand peo - ple, may - be more.
si - lence like a can - cer grows.'

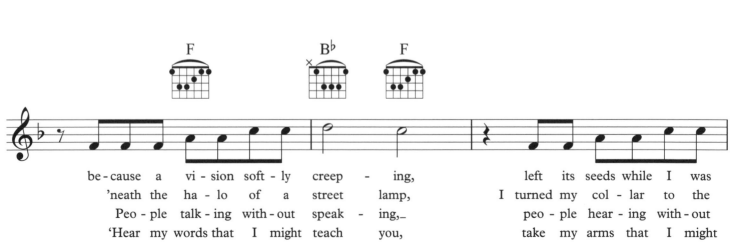

be - cause a vi - sion soft - ly creep - ing,   left its seeds while I was
'neath the ha - lo of a street lamp,   I turned my col - lar to the
Peo - ple talk - ing with - out speak - ing,_   peo - ple hear - ing with - out
'Hear my words that I might teach you,   take my arms that I might

sleep - ing,
cold and damp
lis - ten - ing
reach you'

and the vi - sion_____ that was
when my eyes were stabbed by the
peo - ple writ - ing songs_____ that____
but my words like____

1-3.

plant - ed in my brain still re - mains
flash of a ne - on light that split the night
voi - ces____ nev - er share and no one dare
si - lent rain - drops

with - in the sound of si - lence._____
and touched the sound of si - lence._____
dis - turb the sound of si - lence._____

4.

fell, and ech - oed_____ in the

wells of si - lence._____ 5. And the peo - ple bowed and

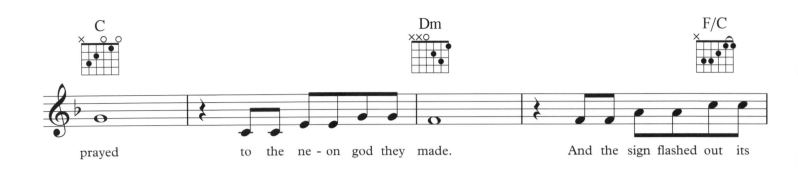

prayed to the ne - on god they made. And the sign flashed out its

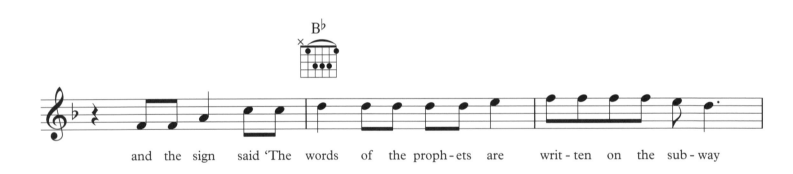

warn - ing,____ in the words that it was form - ing,____

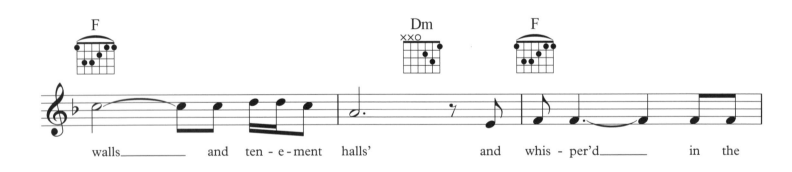

and the sign said 'The words of the proph-ets are writ-ten on the sub-way

walls_____ and ten - e - ment halls' and whis - per'd_____ in the

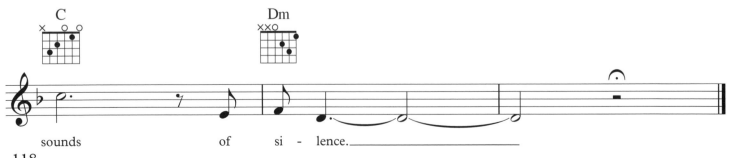

sounds of si - lence._____

118

Tears In Heaven

Words & Music by Eric Clapton & Will Jennings

Picking style:

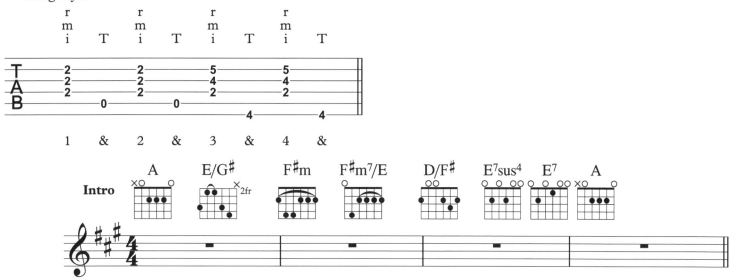

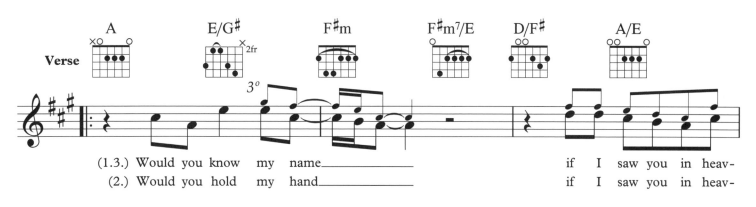

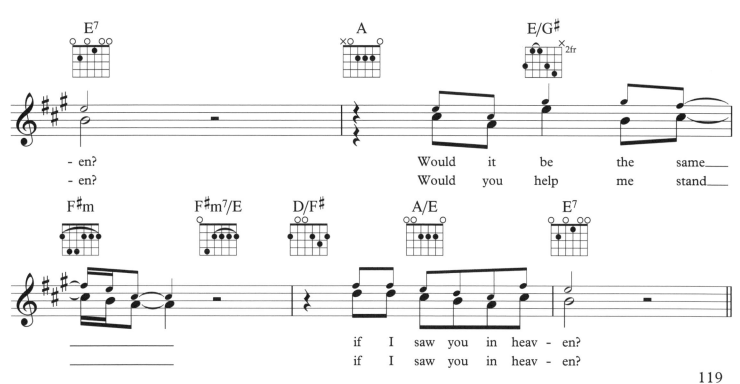

Chorus

F#m   C#7/E#   Em6

(1,4.) I must be strong   and car - ry on
(2.) I'll find my way   through night and day
(3.) Be - yond the door   there's peace I'm sure,

F#7   E/G#   F#/A#   Bm7   Bm7/E

Verse 4 to Coda ⊕

    'cause I know   I don't be - long   here in heav -
    'cause I know   I just can't stay   here in heav -
    and I know   there'll be no more   tears in heav -

1, 3.

A   E/G#   F#m   F#m7/E   D/F#   Esus4   E7   A

- en.
- en.
- en.

2.

Bridge   A   C   G/B   Am7   D/F#

Time can bring you down   time can bend your knees.

G   D/F#   Em7   D/F#   G   C   G/B   Am7

Time can break your heart,

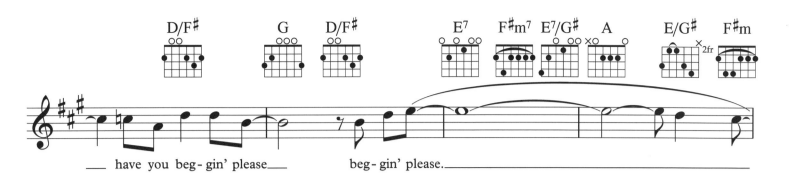

have you beg-gin' please___ beg-gin' please.___

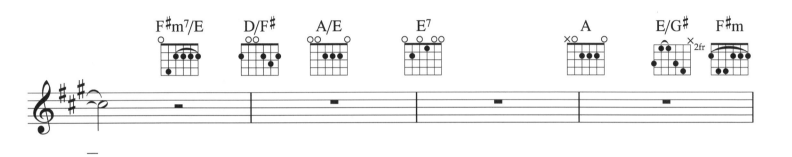

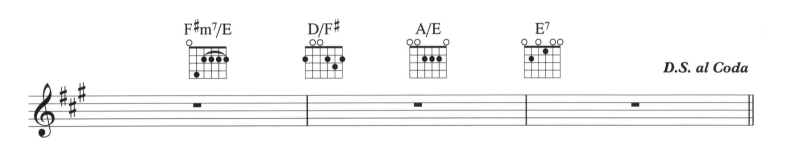

D.S. al Coda

⊕ *Coda*

en. 'Cause I know I don't be-long___ here in heav-

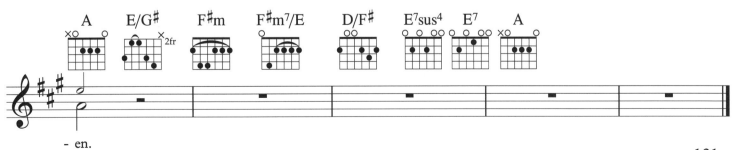

- en.

Torn

Words & Music by Anne Preven, Phil Thornalley & Scott Cutler

no - thing's fine,___ I'm torn.___ I'm___ all out___ of faith,___

___ this___ is how___ I feel,___ I'm cold and I___ am shamed___
4° I'm cold and I'm___ a - shamed___

___ ly - ing na - ked on the floor.___
___ bound and bro - ken on the floor.___ Il - lu - sion nev - er changed___ in - to some - thing real,___

4° Skip to Link

___ wide a - wake and I___ can see___ the per - fect sky___ is torn,___ you're a lit - tle late___

Link

___ I'm al - rea - dy torn.___

D.S. *repeat Chorus*
ad lib. to fade

Torn.___ Ooh___ ooh ooh.___ There's

Verse 2:
So I guess the fortune-teller's right,
I should have seen just what was there
And not some holy light.
But you crawled beneath my veins
And now I don't care I had no luck,
I don't miss it all that much.
There's just so many things
That I can't touch, I'm torn.

Verse 3:
There's nothing where he used to lie,
My inspiration has all run dry,
That's what's going on,
Nothing's right, I'm torn.

123

Vincent (Starry Starry Night)

Words & Music by Don McLean

Picking style:

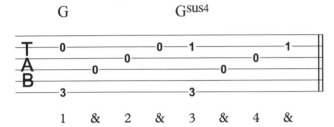

> Try picking like this in the verse, in a crisp, precise fashion—and for a change in dynamics, add simple strumming in eighth-notes in the chorus and bridge.

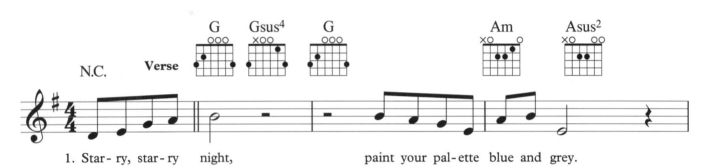

1. Star-ry, star-ry night, paint your pal-ette blue and grey.

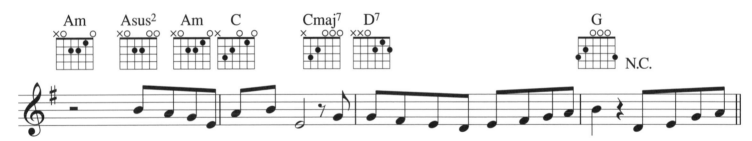

Look out on a sum-mer's day with eyes that know the dark-ness in my soul. Shad-ows on the

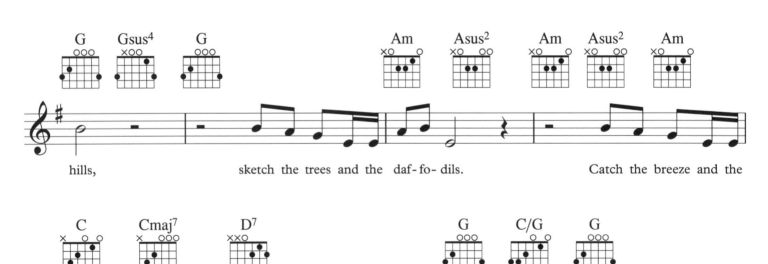

hills, sketch the trees and the daf-fo-dils.

Catch the breeze and the

win-ter chills, in col-ours on the snow-y lin-en land.

Now I un-der-

Chorus

-stand   what you tried   to say   to me,___   and how you suf-fered for your

san - i - ty.___   And how you tried to set them free; they would not lis- ten, they did

not know how,___   per-haps they'll lis-ten   now.___   2. Star-ry, star-ry

Verse

night,   fla - ming flowers that bright-ly blaze.   Swirl - ing clouds in
(3.) night,   por - traits hung   in emp - ty halls.   Frame - less heads on

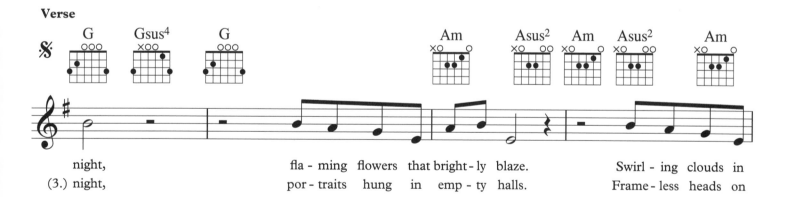

vio - let haze   re - flec-ting Vin-cent's eyes of chi - na blue.   Col - ours chang - ing
name-less walls   with eyes that watch the world and can't for - get. Like the stran-gers that you've

125

hue,
met,
mor-ning fields of am-ber grain.
the rag-ged men in rag-ged clothes.
Weath-ered fa-ces
a sil-ver thorn of

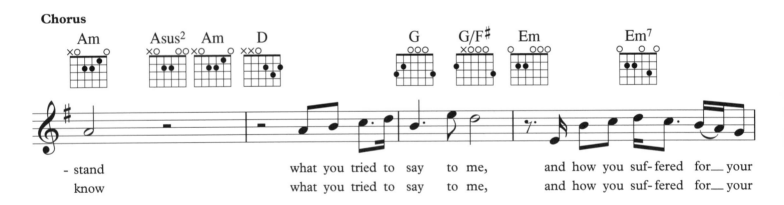

lined in pain__
blood-y rose,__
are soothed be-neath the art-ist's__ lov-ing hand.
lie crushed and bro-ken on the__ vir-gin snow.
Now I un-der-
Now I think I

Chorus

-stand
know
what you tried to say to me,
what you tried to say to me,
and how you suf-fered for__ your
and how you suf-fered for__ your

To Coda ✛

san-i-ty.__
san-i-ty.__
And how you tried to set them free; they would not lis-ten, they did
And how you tried to set them

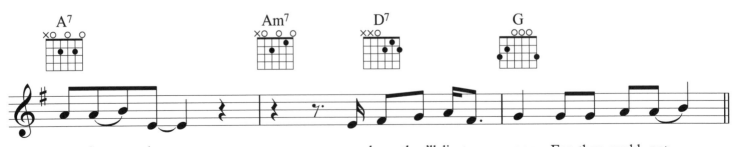

not know__ how,__
per-haps they'll lis-ten now. For they could not__

Bridge

love you,— but still your love was true.—

And when no hope was left in sight,— on that star-ry, star-ry night, you

took your life as lov-ers of-ten do. But I could have told you Vin-cent, this

D.S. al Coda

world was nev-er meant for one as beau-ti-ful— as you. 3. Star-ry star-ry

Coda

free; they would not lis-ten, they're not list-'ning still.— Per-haps they nev-er

will.— *(Guitar)*

127

The Weight

Words & Music by Robbie Robertson (The Band)

Strumming style:

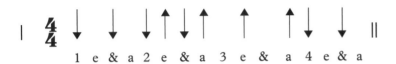

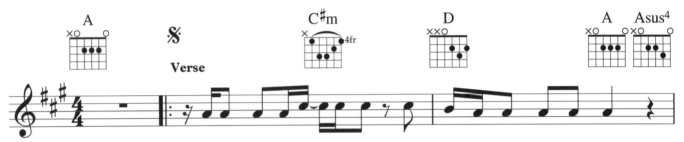

1. I pulled in - to Na - za - reth, was feel - in' 'bout half-past dead.
2. I picked up my bag, I went look - ing for a place to hide,
3. Go down, Miss Mos - es, there's no - thing you can say,

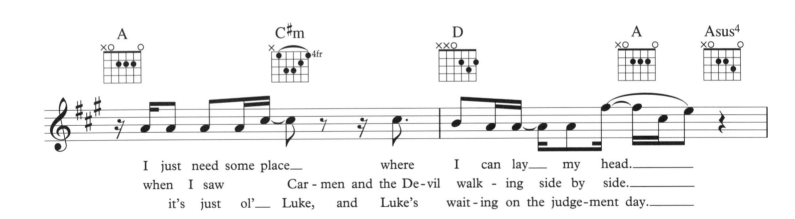

I just need some place where I can lay my head.
when I saw Car - men and the De - vil walk - ing side by side.
it's just ol' Luke, and Luke's wait - ing on the judge - ment day.

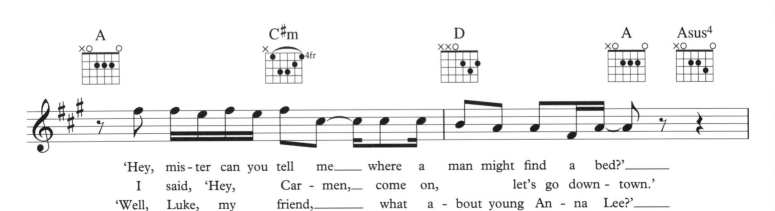

'Hey, mis - ter can you tell me where a man might find a bed?'
I said, 'Hey, Car - men, come on, let's go down - town.'
'Well, Luke, my friend, what a - bout young An - na Lee?'

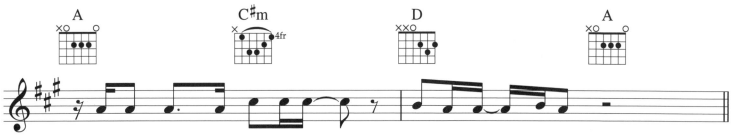

He just grinned and shook my hand,___ 'No' was all___ he said.
She said,___ 'I got - ta go, but my friend can stick a round.
He said, 'Do me a fa - vour son,_ won't you stay and keep An - na Lee com - pa - ny?'

Chorus

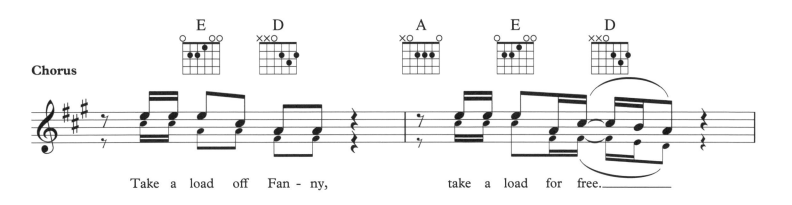

Take a load off Fan - ny, take a load for free.___

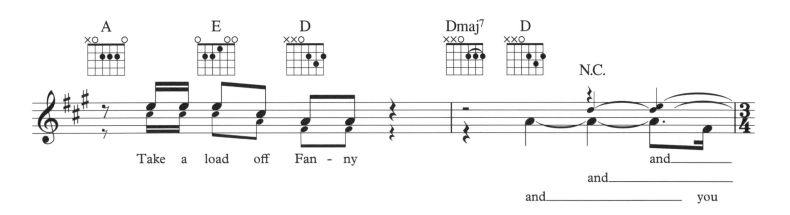

Take a load off Fan - ny
and___
and___
and___ you

1-3.

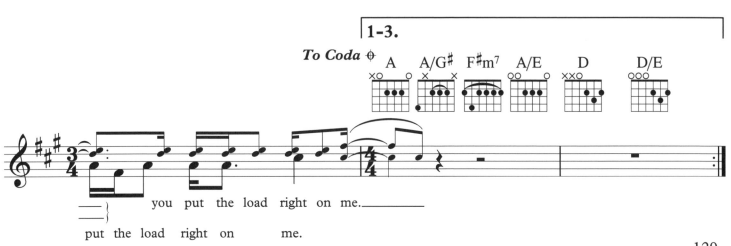

To Coda ⊕

___ you put the load right on me.___
put the load right on me.

129

Verse 4
Crazy Chester followed me and he caught me in the fog.
He said, 'I will fix your rack if you take Jack, my dog.'
I said, 'Wait a minute, Chester, you know, I'm a peaceful man.'
He said, 'That's okay boy, won't you feed him when you can?'

Take a load off, Fanny etc.

Verse 5
Catch a cannonball, now, to take me down the line.
My bag is sinking low and I do believe it's time
To get back to Miss Fanny, you know, she's the only one
Who sent me here with her regards for everyone.

Take a load off, Fanny etc.

Wild World

Words & Music by Cat Stevens

Strumming style:

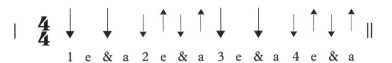

1 e & a 2 e & a 3 e & a 4 e & a

> Strum two accented eighth-notes followed by a group of four sixteenth-notes, as shown, for a flowing feel to the rhythm.

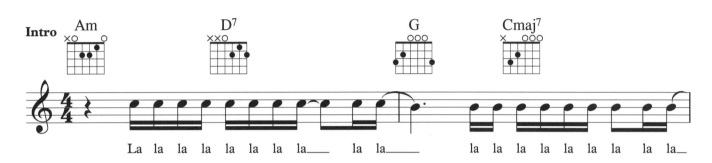

Intro

La la la la la la la la___ la la___ la la la la la la la la la___

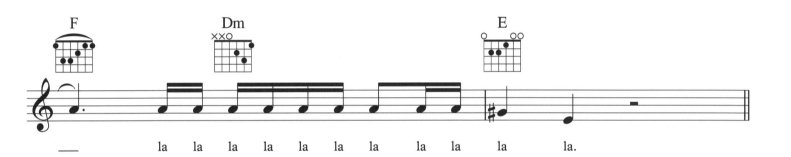

___ la la la la la la la la la la la.

Verse

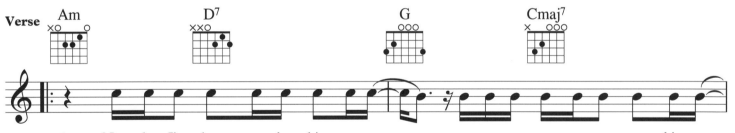

1. Now that I've lost ev-'ry-thing to you___ you say you wan-na start some-thing new___
2. You know I've seen a lot of what the world can do___ and it's break-ing my heart in two___

___ and it's break-ing my heart__ you're leav - ing. Ba - by I'm griev - in'!
___ be - cause I ne - ver want to see you sad, girl. Don't be a bad__ girl.

131

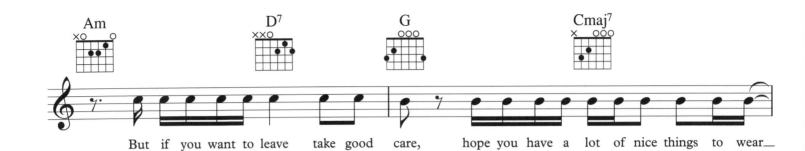

But if you want to leave take good care, hope you have a lot of nice things to wear___
But if you want to leave take good care, hope you make a lot of nice friends out there___

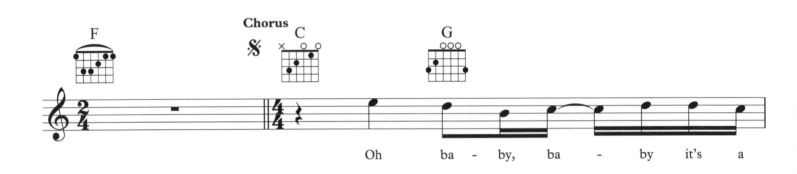

___ but then a lot of nice things turn bad out there___
___ but just re-mem-ber there's a lot of bad and be - ware___

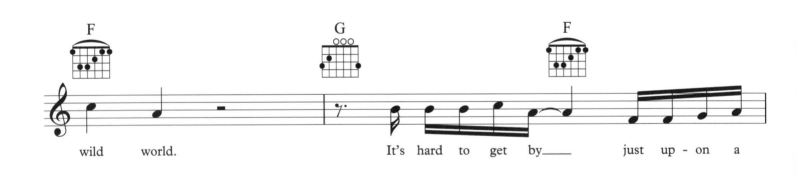

Chorus

Oh ba - by, ba - by it's a

wild world.   It's hard to get by___ just up - on a

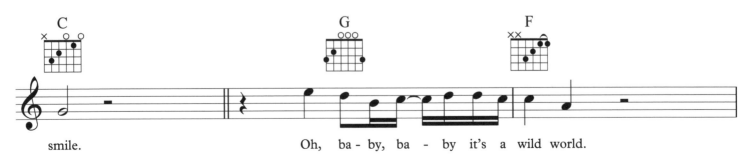

smile.   Oh, ba - by, ba - by it's a wild world.

132

I'll al-ways re-mem-ber you____ like a child, girl.____

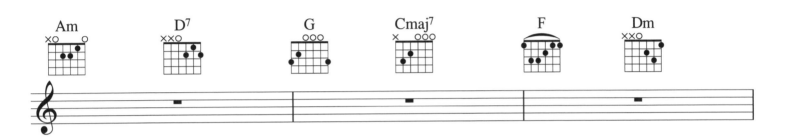

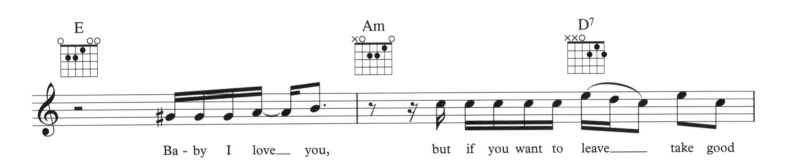

Ba - by I love____ you, but if you want to leave____ take good

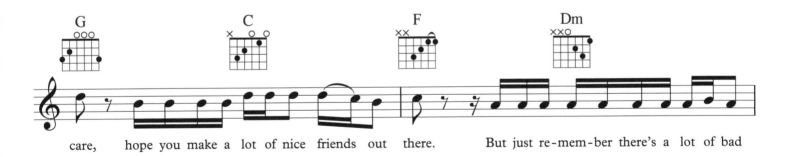

care, hope you make a lot of nice friends out there. But just re-mem-ber there's a lot of bad

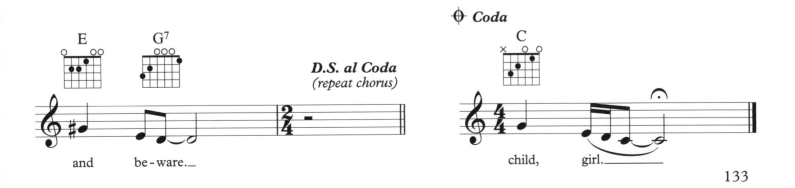

D.S. al Coda
(repeat chorus)

and be-ware.____

child, girl.____

133

Wonderwall

Words & Music by Noel Gallagher

Strumming style:

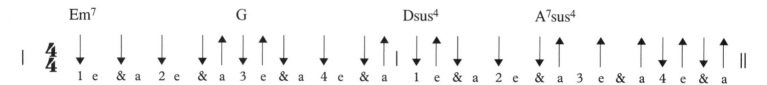

Capo: Fret 2

Intro

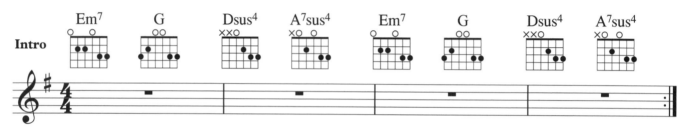

Verse

1. To - day   is   gon - na be the day that they're gon-na throw it   back to   you.__
2. Back-beat   the word was on the street that   the   fi - re   in your heart is   out.__
3. To - day   was gon - na be the day but they'll nev - er throw it   back to   you.__

By   now   you should-'ve some-how re - al - ised   what   you got - ta do.__
I'm sure you've heard it   all before but you   nev - er real - ly had a doubt.
By   now   you should-'ve some-how re - al - ised   what you're not   to do.__

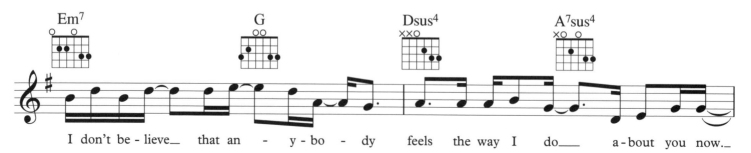

I don't be - lieve__ that an - y - bo - dy   feels the way I do__ a - bout you now.__

134

You're Still The One

Words & Music by Shania Twain & R.J. Lange

Strumming style:

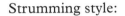

Capo: Fret 1

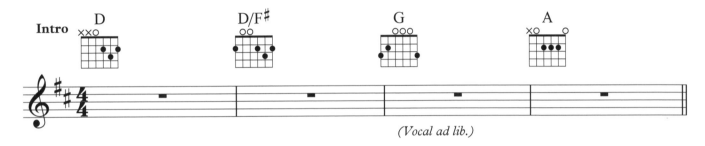

(Vocal ad lib.)

1. Looks like we made___ it,_____ look how far___ we've come_
2. Ain't noth-ing bet-ter,_____ we beat___ the odds_

___ my ba - by._____ We might have took the long___ way,_____
___ to-geth-er._____ I'm glad we did-n't list - en,_____

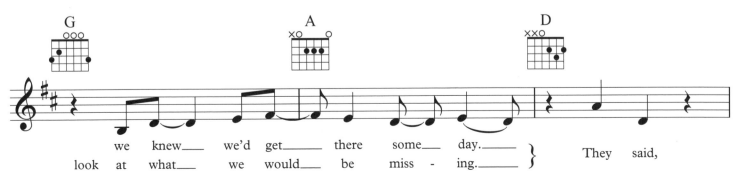

we knew___ we'd get_____ there some___ day._____ } They said,
look at what___ we would___ be miss-ing._____

I bet, they'll nev - er make____ it, but just

look at____ us hold - ing____ on,____ we're still to - geth -

- er, still go - ing____ strong.____ (Still the one.)

Chorus

You're still the one I____ run____ to____ the one that I be - long____

____ to._____ You're still the one I want____ for

life. (Still the one.) You're still the one that____ I____

G   Em⁷   A

love,____   the on-ly one I____ dream____ of,_____

D   G

you're still the one I kiss good

|1.
A

To Coda ⊕

night.

|2.
A

You're still____ the one.

D   G   A   D.S. al Coda

(Still the one.)

⊕ Coda
A   D   D/F♯

I'm so glad we made____ it,

G   A

look how far____ we've come my ba - by.

Yesterday

Words & Music by John Lennon & Paul McCartney

Picking style:

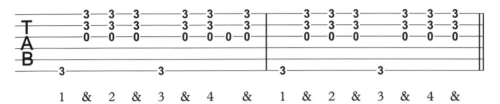

To match original recording, tune down one tone.

Intro

Verse

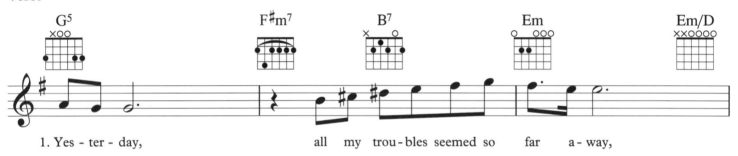

1. Yes - ter - day,   all my trou - bles seemed so far a - way,

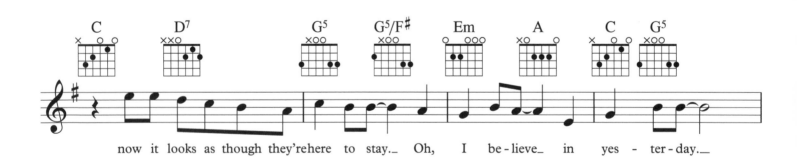

now it looks as though they're here to stay._ Oh, I be - lieve_ in yes - ter - day._

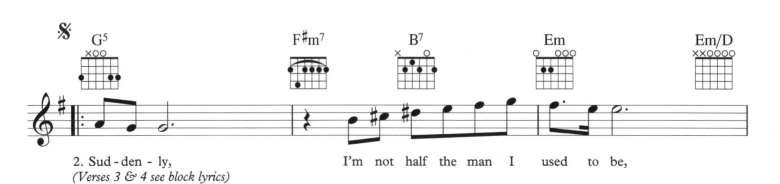

2. Sud - den - ly,   I'm not half the man I used to be,
(Verses 3 & 4 see block lyrics)

there's a sha-dow hang-ing o-ver me.___ Oh, yes-ter-day___ came

Bridge

sud-den-ly.___ Why she had to go I don't

know, she would-n't say.___ I said

1. 2.

D.S. al Coda

some-thing wrong, now I long for yes-ter-day.___ - day.___

⊕ *Coda*

yes-ter-day.___ Mm, mm, mm, mm, mm, mm, mm.___

Verses 3 & 4:
Yesterday, love was such an easy game to play,
Now I need a place to hide away.
Oh, I believe in yesterday.

You've Got A Friend

Words & Music by Carole King

Picking style:

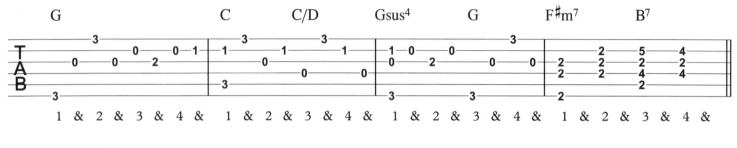

Capo: Fret 2

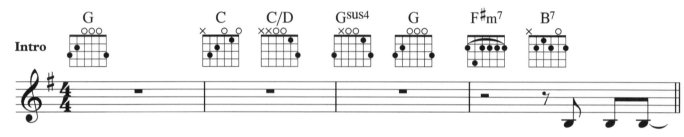

Intro

1. When you're down_

Verse

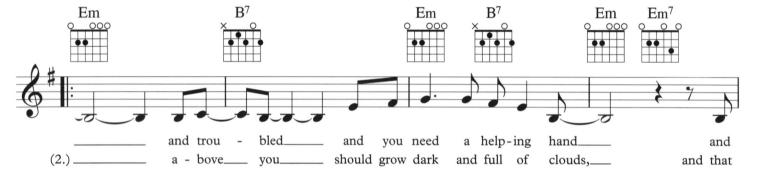

_____ and trou - bled_____ and you need a help-ing hand_____ and

(2.) _____ a - bove_____ you_____ should grow dark and full of clouds,_____ and that

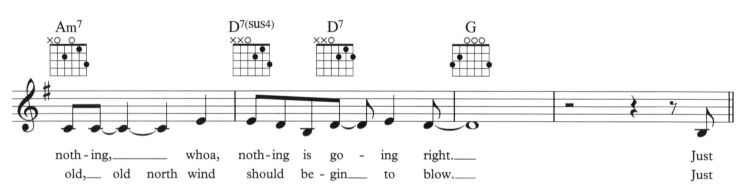

noth - ing,_____ whoa, noth-ing is go - ing right._____ Just

old,_ old north wind should be - gin to blow._____ Just

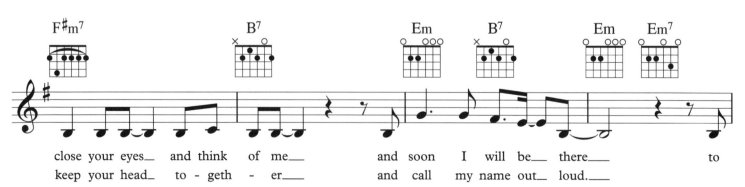

close your eyes_ and think of me_ and soon I will be there_ to

keep your head_ to - geth - er_____ and call my name out_ loud._____

bright-ten up___ e - ven your dark - est nights.___ }
Soon you'll hear me knock - ing____ on__ your door.___ }

You just call__

𝄋 Chorus

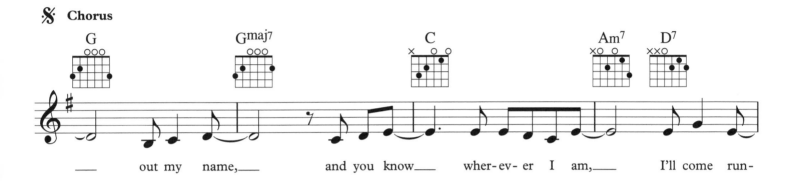

__ out my name,___ and you know___ wher-ev- er I am,___ I'll come run-

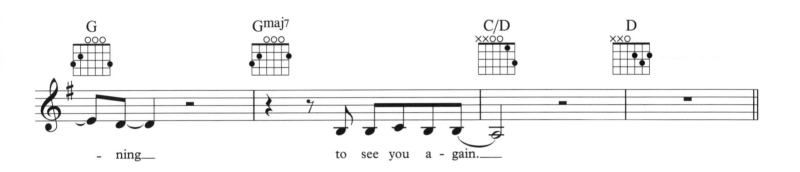

- ning___ to see you a - gain.___

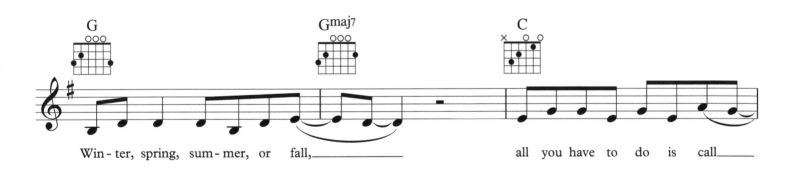

Win - ter, spring, sum-mer, or fall,_____ all you have to do is call___

To Coda ⊕ |**1.**

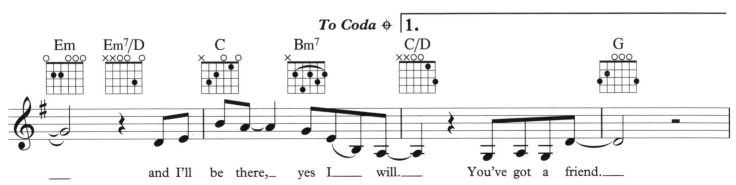

and I'll be there,_ yes I__ will.__ You've got a friend.__